Twentieth Century Architecture 8

Twentieth Century Architecture 8

EDITED BY SUSANNAH CHARLTON
ELAIN HARWOOD AND ALAN POWERS

BRITISH MODERN

ARCHITECTURE AND DESIGN IN THE 1930s

The Twentieth Century Society
2007

TWENTIETH CENTURY ARCHITECTURE
is published by the Twentieth Century Society
70 Cowcross Street, London EC1M 6EJ
© The authors 2007
The views expressed in *British Modern: Architecture and Design in the 1930s* are those of the authors, and not necessarily those of the Twentieth Century Society.

NUMBER 8 | 2007 | ISBN 0 9529755–8–0

Twentieth Century Architecture Editorial Committee:
Susannah Charlton, Elain Harwood, Alan Powers,
Gavin Stamp and Simon Wartnaby. Sarah Yates assisted
with editing.

Designed by Dalrymple
Typeset in Utopia and Penumbra
Printed by Henry Ling Limited

The Twentieth Century Society has received a bequest from
Catherine Cooke and generous grants from The Marc Fitch
Fund, The John Anstey Foundation and English Heritage
towards the cost of this publication. The society also gratefully
acknowledges a grant from English Heritage towards the cost
of its casework, and Sophie Bowness and Christ's College,
Cambridge, for help with photography.

ENGLISH HERITAGE

The Twentieth Century Society was founded in 1979 to
promote and preserve architecture and design from 1914
onwards. For information and membership details call
+44 (0)20 7250 3857 or contact www.c20society.org.uk.

The frontispiece is Dell and Wainwright's view of the *Daily
Express* Building by Sir Owen Williams of 1931. (Architecural
Press Archive / RIBA Library Photographs Collection, with
thanks to Robert Elwall).

CONTENTS

CONTRIBUTORS

JOHN ALLAN, a Director of Avanti Architects, has led a series of Modern Movement restoration projects and studies, including buildings by Lubetkin, Lasdun, Goldfinger, Patrick Gwynne, LCC, Oliver Hill, Connell, Ward & Lucas, Wells Coates, Maxwell Fry, Peter Moro, Burnet Tait & Lorne, Owen Williams, David Roberts, and Maguire & Murray. Publications include *Berthold Lubetkin: Architecture and the Tradition of Progress*, RIBA Publications 1992; 'The Conservation of Modern Buildings', in *Building Maintenance & Preservation*, 2nd Edition, Butterworth-Heinemann 1994; *Berthold Lubetkin*, Merrell 2002.

BARNABAS CALDER is working for the RIBA Drawings & Archives Collections, cataloguing the archive of Sir Denys Lasdun. He has recently completed a PhD thesis within the Cambridge University Department of Architecture on Lasdun's National Theatre.

BRIDGET CHERRY began working on *The Buildings of England* in 1968 as Pevsner's research assistant. From 1971 to 2002 she was editor of what are now called the *Pevsner Architectural Guides*, and established their present format with *London 2: South* in 1983. She has since revised Londons 3, 4 and 5, the latter with Charles O'Brien, and *Devon*. She has also served as a commissioner for both English Heritage and the Royal Commission on Historical Monuments of England, and is Vice Chair of the Twentieth Century Society.

DENIS CLARKE HALL (1910–2006) discovered modern architecture in 1934–5 when he was a student at the Architectural Association. His career was spectacularly launched when aged 26 he won the *News Chronicle* competition for a secondary school in 1937. The modern design was carefully underpinned on scientific principles for ensuring natural light and noise separation in the classrooms, and Clarke Hall went on to design 26 more schools, as well as public housing and civic centres.

ELIZABETH DARLING is an architectural historian and a senior lecturer at the Department of History of Art at Oxford Brookes University. She researches and publishes on gender, housing and modernism, particularly in inter-war Britain. Her book, *Re-forming Britain: Narratives of Modernity before Reconstruction* is published by Routledge in 2006.

ROBERT ELWALL is Photographs Curator of the British Architectural Library, RIBA. His publications include *Building with Light: the International History of Architectural Photography* (2004) and *Photography Takes Command: the Camera and British Architecture 1890–1939* (1994). His book on the photographer Edwin Smith will appear in Spring 2007.

ROYSTON FOOT studied engineering after serving in the Royal Navy. He worked for the London County Council before joining Sir Owen Williams and Partners in 1956, where he became a partner in 1962, retiring as Managing Partner in 1992. He was responsible for a number of industrial buildings, several associated with the newspaper industry, and had wide experience of the structural design of bridges and viaducts.

SIR NIKOLAUS PEVSNER (1902–83), established his career as an art and architectural historian in Germany before moving to Britain in 1933. He later became Professor of History of Art at Birkbeck College (University of London), Slade Professor of Fine Art at Cambridge and an RIBA Gold Medallist. In addition to *The Buildings of England*, first published from 1951 to 1974, he was founding editor of *The Pelican History of Art* and of *The Buildings of Ireland, Scotland and Wales*.

CHRIS STEPHENS is a Curator of Modern British Art and Head of Collection Displays at Tate Britain. Specialising in the art of St Ives in the 1940s and 1950s and modern British sculpture, he has published books and articles on Barbara Hepworth, Peter Lanyon, Hubert Dalwood, Terry Frost, Bryan Wynter. He has books forthcoming on Brian Wall and Roger Hilton and is working on a new critical history of art in St Ives 1939–75. He curated the Barbara Hepworth centenary exhibition at Tate St Ives in 2003 and *This was Tomorrow: Art and the Sixties* and *Gwen John and Augustus John* at Tate Britain, both in 2004.

FOREWORD

All but one of the essays in this collection began life as conference papers in March 1999. The two-day event was organised jointly by the Twentieth Century Society and the Design Museum, which was then showing the exhibition *Modern Britain 1929–39*, curated by James Peto and Donna Loveday, with Judith Collins and myself as consultant curators.

The purpose of the exhibition was to show the links between 'fine art' and design during the period, within the accepted definition of 'modern'. It happened to be twenty years on from the *Thirties* exhibition organised by the Arts Council at the Hayward Gallery. In retrospect, the much larger 1979 exhibition was, in its pluralism, a symptom of the rise of post-modernism. In 1999, the mood was 'Cool Britannia', and it seemed appropriate to look back and see the 1930s as a precursor to New Labour Britain's growing self-confidence as a centre of design. Texts of the period by Herbert Read and others made the assumption (shared by the Bauhaus) that abstract artists would be the most appropriate 'form givers' for industrial design, releasing a spiritual jolt to the depressed nation through mass-produced objects. At the same time, artists led the way in other directions where their influence may have been more profound, towards a love of the countryside, of traditional crafts, and a realisation that real modernism in Britain might perhaps have happened a thousand years earlier, before the Norman Conquest.

Several of the essays in the catalogue developed this theme, and the displays, organised in a roughly chronological sequence, planted the germ of Surrealism at the far end of the room (around the year 1935), so that one could watch it germinating in the romanticism of the second half of the decade. By 1939, something different to the smooth machine forms of Highpoint I caused the cowhide chairs from Lubetkin's penthouse at Highpoint 2, which were shown in a recessed room. John Piper's watercolour of Regency Brighton owned by Wells Coates came afterwards, to indicate a romantic turn to nostalgia and the final object was Graham Sutherland's *Entrance to a Lane, Pembrokeshire*, painted at the time that the war broke out. This paired with Paul Nash's *Dead Spring*, 1929, the first object in the exhibition, and the implication was meant to be that the Waste Land of post-industrial Britain had come into rich green leafage over the course of ten years – not quite the standard narrative of modernism.

Some items – Isokon furniture, the London Transport map, the model of the De La Warr Pavilion and Keith Murray pots – virtually selected themselves (provided loans could be agreed). There was not enough space for all the textiles requested from Manchester Art Gallery in the elegant design undulating wall design by Norman Foster, but there was a small section on health buildings, one on children's art and another on Dartington Hall. Some items from private collections were exhibited for the first time. The newsreel style presentation made for a popular exhibition, which seemed able to communicate the ambiguities of modernism in the period as well as the certainties.

The conference was an attempt to fill some of the gaps and develop the

main theme of art and design connections. It was a particular pleasure to have as speakers two architects who had each completed significant buildings in the 1930s: Sir Denys Lasdun and Denis Clarke Hall. The former spoke informally, and did not wish his paper to be published, and is therefore represented here by Barnabas Calder's account of his pre-war career.

Regrettably, it has not been possible to include all the conference papers here, owing to constraints of space and the need to focus on architecture. Those omitted were: David Peters-Corbett on Wyndham Lewis; Martin Hammer on Naum Gabo; Lucy Pratt on Ben Nicholson's textiles, Fiona Russell on Ruskin in the 1930s; Lynda Morris on Frederic Antal and émigré realism; David Dewing on the new 1930s room at the Geffrye Museum, Cheryl Buckley on Susie Cooper, and John Hewitt on Shell Advertising. Most of these contributors have published related texts before or since the conference, but they deserve thanks for preparing their material for print following the event.

After the conference, kind members of the audience said that a book should be made from it, little knowing the difficulties involved. First of all, Caroline Boileau, then a committee member of the Twentieth Century Society, assembled texts and illustrations from the speakers, transcribing from tapes where necessary. The Society first considered a less polished form of publication than the present one, and Suzanne Gorman, then my colleague at the Prince of Wales's Institute of Architecture, generously embarked on a layout. Owing to the other publishing priorities of the Society, it was not possible then to proceed further, but knowing the scarcity of new scholarship and documentation in this field, it is a great pleasure now to bring all this work to fruition.

In 2006, the exhibition *Modernism, Making a New World 1914–1939* curated by Christopher Wilk at the V&A has presented the British public with an international context for what was explored at the Design Museum seven years previously, showing that the period is still alive with controversial interpretations. It remains difficult to insert Britain into the international narrative, but we believe that the text by Sir Nikolaus Pevsner, published here for the first time, brings a fresh and non-parochial voice from the past, encouraging a new look at the canon of British Modernist architecture and its relationship with the wider field. We are grateful to Susie Harries for providing a copy of the original typescript in the Getty Center, California, who, with Dieter Pevsner, have given permission to publish it here. Elain Harwood contributed the footnotes identifying the buildings.

Susannah Charlton has done the bulk of the editorial work, with help from Elain Harwood, Simon Wartnaby and Sarah Yates. Morley von Sternberg has kindly permitted use of his photograph of White House, Haslemere on the cover, taken for the book *Modern: the Modern Movement* in Britain, featuring his photographs with my text, published in 2005 by Merrell.

As on previous occasions, we are extremely grateful to English Heritage for contributing to the costs. The late Dr Catherine Cooke, architect and historian of Russian modernism, a former member of the Twentieth Century Society committee and a doughty chair of DOCOMOMO UK generously left a benefaction of £2000 to the Society in her will. Her gift has been used for the production of this book and it is dedicated to her memory.

Left: Detail from the exhibition *Modern Britain* held at the Design Museum in 1999.
Overleaf: Connell, Ward and Lucas, 66 Frognal, Hampstead, 1937.

1 THE MODERN MOVEMENT IN BRITAIN

NIKOLAUS PEVSNER

THE MODERN MOVEMENT IN BRITAIN

INTRODUCTION BY BRIDGET CHERRY

When Nikolaus Pevsner moved to England in 1933 at the age of 31 he had already established himself in his native Germany as an art historian with wide interests. His early studies on the Baroque style had resulted in a book on the Baroque houses of Leipzig and an authoritative survey of Italian Mannerist and Baroque painting[1]. These followed the tradition of lively interest by German art historians in the relationship of Northern European and Italian art of the seventeenth century, and the relatively recent acceptance (which developed in parallel with the growth of a unified Germany), that German seventeenth- and eighteenth-century Baroque was a form of art worthy of merit on its own terms. But already in the later 1920s, Pevsner's interests were turning to subjects outside the realm of traditional academic art history, the relationship of present-day art and architecture to the past, and the changing position of the artist and architect in society.[2] At the same time he was developing an interest in English art and architecture, giving lectures on this subject to an English circle at Göttingen University. He had visited England already in 1930 to collect material for this. However, as he was aware before he finally left Germany, English traditions were not sympathetic either to modernism or to academic art history, and architectural history tended to be written by traditional-minded architects.[3] As Pevsner recalled later, on his arrival he found contemporary British architecture 'very reactionary'.[4] Twentieth-century Britain offered challenges both to the interpreter and to the critic.

German art history, established as an academic subject already in the nineteenth century, had developed an impressive tradition of analysis and documentary research, but also embraced the history of ideas, which involved grappling with broad philosophical and historical themes and theories. The evolution of style was a key issue. Did styles have a natural (and perhaps inevitable) rise, maturity and decline, as was sometimes the assumption of older historians, or, as was debated by Pevsner's supervisor, the charismatic and controversial Wilhelm Pinder, did new styles evolve in reaction to those of older generations, could several styles develop simultaneously, and to what extent did styles relate to the thorny question of 'national character'?[5] Pevsner was not unaffected by these arguments and, although he was not essentially a theorist, his writings show traces of such considerations.[6] His interest in broad themes is apparent in his most celebrated pre-war book, *Pioneers of Modern Design from William Morris to Walter Gropius* (1936), which provided antecedents in nineteenth-century England for the principles of modernism. This shows Pevsner's ability to bind together disparate elements into a coherent, if selective, narrative. But although Pevsner makes clear that he sees the modernism of the Bauhaus as the appropriate style for the twentieth century, its work is not described in *Pioneers*, which stops on the threshold of the new era. His other book from this time, *An Enquiry into Industrial Art in England* (1937), written when he was a research assistant attached to Birmingham University, explores the character and reasons for bad contemporary industrial art but

1. *Leipziger Barock, Der Baukunst der Barockzeit in Leipzig*, 1928; *Barockmalerei in den remanischen Ländern. I Die italienische Malerei vom Ende der Renaissance bis zum augehenden Rokoko*, 1928.

2. On Pevsner's early intellectual development see Peter Draper, ed., *Reassessing Nikolaus Pevsner*, 2004, especially Paul Crossley, Introduction, and Ute Engel, 'The formation of Pevsner's art history: Nikolaus Pevsner in Germany 1902–1935'.

3. See his critical review of M. Briggs, 'The architect in history', 1927, in *Kritische Berichte zur Kunstgeschichtlichen Literatur* 3 / 4 1930–1, pp.97–121, where he observes that Sir Reginald Blomfield, one of the leaders of the 'neuenglischen imperialischen Bau-Klassizismus' was also the author of numerous textbooks on English and French Renaissance architecture.

4. Nikolaus Pevsner, 'Zehn Jahre Bauen in Grossbritannien (1924–1934)', *Bauen+Wohnen*, 1964, pp.461–3.

5. M. Halbertsma, *Wilhelm Pinder und die deutsche Kunstgeschichte*, 1992.

6. For a discussion of German art historical influences on Pevsner see S. Muthesius, 'Germanness, Englishness, Jewishness, scientificness, popularisation', in *Reassessing Nikolaus Pevsner, op.cit.*, pp. 59–69

similarly does not analyse the nature of good design. However, it led to a number of articles by Pevsner on contemporary design which were published in the *Architectural Review*, and it was the *Review* which offered him an opportunity to pursue further the subject of the development of twentieth-century architecture in Britain. Here was the chance, drawing on his considerable knowledge of recent architecture, to describe the multiplicity of current styles in his adopted country, to assess the impact on them of the Modern Movement, and point a way to the future. In 1938–9 he planned a special issue for December 1939 which was to be devoted to the subject. His introduction explains that it was to be 'an attempt to take stock of the architectural landscape as it presents itself to the public, that is to say, as regards the appearance of buildings'. It continues:

> *Architects each with a consistent set of mannerisms, are always competing for public patronage. But this battle differs from the 'Battles of the Styles' fought in the nineteenth century, in that two 'pure' styles revived from previous epochs have given way to a number of 'impure' styles, each recognisable by dominant characteristics but each consisting of an idiom built up from various sources. Moreover the 'modern' idiom, having started as a functionalist rebellion against the purely stylistic idea of architecture and now tending to crystallise itself as a new 'contemporary' style, has considerably influenced other styles current today. In fact a revolution in architecture has taken place, due to the infiltration of 'modern' ideas and their adoption, consciously or unconsciously, by all kinds of architects.*

His purpose was to classify these different styles – and then to show that there was the potential for a specifically British brand of the new style. He aimed to provide 'a clearer vision of the Modern Movement in its architectural elements, and a clearer vision of the British national character in its architectural expression' so that 'it should not be impossible to arrive in the end at a vista towards a wholly British and wholly contemporary style of the future whose first examples are perhaps already in existence.'

What is presented here is the essay on the Modern Movement, setting 'progressive' British buildings from the 1920s to 1939 in the context of developments abroad. It survives as a corrected but unedited typescript in the Pevsner archive at the Getty Center, Los Angeles, together with the drafts of essays on the other twentieth-century stylistic categories which he identified: these included thorough discussions of 'British imperial' (subdivided into three groups); Neo-Georgian, official and commercial; architectural historicism, Gothic and Tudor; Renaissance, northern and southern; and two stages of Swedish influence.

The essays were completed in typescript, with some handwritten corrections but no indication about illustrations. The outbreak of war in September 1939 ended plans for the special issue. After the war Pevsner became preoccupied with other matters and his account of British twentieth-century architecture remained unpublished, although he drew on some of the general comments when he came to write *The Englishness of English Art* (1956), and a short account of 1920s architecture in Britain published in German in 1964. [7]

Pevsner's effort at providing a synthetic account of twentieth-century British architecture up to 1939, based on abstract stylistic analysis and seen from the point of view of the spectator, stood apart from contemporary architectural criticism, which was more often concerned to discuss individual buildings and architects, with an emphasis on planning and building materials.[8] In a rare later essay on theory, Pevsner deplored the lack of intellectual rigour among critics, his comments reflecting the dissatisfaction of a continental art historian whose discipline was still in 1951 barely established in England:

> *The proportions, the lines, the relations of buildings and details today can*

7. See note 4.

8. See for example Charles Marriott, *Modern English Architecture*, 1924; Charles Reilly, *Representative architects of the present day*, 1931

*be described and compared, and also paralleled with other fields, litera-
ture, music and politics. Their unity of twentieth-century language and
purpose could be brought out, if architectural critics made the effort and
applied to buildings of today what instruments have been shaped and
sharpened to deal with buildings of the past.*[9]

In that article, provoked by debates on Coventry Cathedral and the rebuilding
of the House of Commons, his view of style was that it 'takes on the whole of a
personality and the spirit of an age'; for him the new Coventry was 'an expression of the age that was building it', while Giles Scott's rebuilt House of Commons was 'in the style of its designer'. For Pevsner, it was a disappointment
that the Modern Movement had failed to make more headway by 1951, and his
writing during the 50s reflects this. By the later 1960s he was out of sympathy
with recent trends in contemporary architecture, and he also acknowledged
the limitations of his earlier interpretations.[10] But in 1939 he was not yet disil-
lusioned, and his discussion of the varied facets of twentieth-century architecture, which he had skipped over in *Pioneers,* displays a wide-ranging and
optimistic curiosity as to how modern architecture was developing.

BRIDGET CHERRY

9. 'Canons of Criticism', *Architectural Review,* vol.109, no.649, January 1951, pp.3–6

10. Bridget Cherry, '"The Pevsner 50": Nikolaus Pevsner and the listing of modern buildings', *Ancient Monuments Society Transactions,* no.46, 2002, p.101.

EDITORIAL NOTE

Some minor tidying up has been done to Pevsner's unedited typescript, re-
moving references that appeared to be Pevsner's reminders to himself, and
correcting and supplying missing names or dates where possible. For consistency, fuller references to buildings are included in footnotes. Buildings have
been selected for illustration on the principle of preferring the obscure to the
well known.

THE MODERN MOVEMENT IN BRITAIN

NIKOLAUS PEVSNER

I need not be repeated here that the Modern Movement, i.e. a style of the twentieth century completely independent of the past, originated during the last years of Queen Victoria's reign, mainly in Britain, and that, shortly after 1900, a few French and a larger number of German architects took the lead in developing it.

Consequently there was a possibility before the war already of forms of the Modern Movement reaching this country from the continent. One case in particular must be noted.

THE MESSEL-MOTIF IN COMMERCIAL BUILDING

Alfred Messel, who had been one of the first to see the aesthetic possibilities of steel and glass for store buildings, added to his Wertheim Store at Berlin in 1904 an entrance wing for which he seems to have created the motif of a sequence of strongly projecting uprights from the bottom to the top of the building, between which a number of narrow windows, three or four to each bay, are inserted, again separated from each other by less projecting uprights. Thus, except for the line between ground floor and upper floors and the top cornice, no horizontal appears, all the emphasis being laid on short, as it were hammering rhythm verticals. Messel felt the affinity of such a treatment with Gothic principles and did not entirely keep away from gothicizing details. A few years later Josef Olbrich, an Austrian and a pupil of Otto Wagner, evolved a modern version of the theme. His Tietz Store at Dusseldorf of 1908 remained the standard work of the type.

The first English case of a possible dependence on this type seems to be Niven and Falkner's building, Nos.19–21 Hatton Garden, of 1912.[1] Better known

Figure 1. Charles Holden (Adams, Holden and Pearson), London Passenger Transport Board headquarters, 55 Broadway, Westminster, 1927–9

Figure 2. Niven and Wigglesworth, 19–21 Hatton Garden, 1912

Figure 3. Alfred Messel, Wertheim store, Berlin, 1904

1. Normally credited as Niven and Wigglesworth. Harold Falkner was a partner of the firm in 1900–3.

in this connection is Smith & Brewer's new building for Heal's, opened in 1916. From Heal's the motif migrated to several post-war stores and office-buildings such as Bourne & Hollingsworth's in Oxford Street, Leith House in Gresham Street, and also, to quote one recent case, D. H. Evans in Oxford Street.[2]

More often, however, a similar effect of strict verticalism is obtained without introducing a rhythmical fenestration, simply by alternating between uninterrupted uprights and somewhat recessed windows. It can hardly be ascertained where this motif comes from. Peter Behrens has used it in his Volta Street Factory for the AEG in Berlin in 1912, and Cass Gilbert for his Brooklyn Army Stores in 1916. Its earliest appearance is probably in Frank Lloyd Wright's Larkin Building at Buffalo, 1903.

One may assume that some relation exists between such buildings and Sir John Burnet's Adelaide House, completed in 1924. The *Architectural Review* of that year alleged something of a 'sombre influence of Munich' and, in the *Architects' Journal*, Mr Howard Robertson said that 'the design had been criticised as revealing German influences'. He does not seem to believe in these, and he was in my opinion right. There is more of an American accent in

Adelaide House, if any foreign accent there is, than a German. The architect for the Kodak Building and the Cathcart Tailoring Institute can very well have been more able to attain this impressive form for an office building quite independently. Details above all such as the short stylised columns, the zig-zag ornament, and some of the vaguely Egyptian features are entirely un-German.

Adelaide House has had a great effect on British office buildings. It is responsible for the predominance of the uniform fenestration as against Messel's and Olbrich's rhythm. Its influence is particularly distinct in the case of one of Mr Emberton's earliest works, the offices of Austin Reed's in Red Lion Square. It seems also to recur in certain features of Mr Holden's Underground Building. As a rule, however, it is modified by the introduction of a motif which Sir John Burnet has also been one of the first to use in England, the vertical row of metal windows with metal strips in between. This motif which has been discussed in connection with Selfridge's and the Kodak Building became soon popular for the pompous office buildings of the Kingsway and the Regent Street type, columns or pilasters separating the

2. Slater and Moberly, Bourne and Hollingsworth, 1925–7; Richardson and Gill, Leith House, Gresham Street, 1924–6 (demolished); Louis Blanc, D. H. Evans, Oxford Street, 1935–7.

Clockwise from top left

Figure 10. J. H. Markham (Office of Works), British Library Newspaper Library, Colindale Avenue, Hendon, enlarged 1930–2

Figure 11. Gordon Jeeves and H. A. Welch, Everyman House (Drage's), Oxford Street, Westminster, 1929–30

Figure 12. Gordon Jeeves and Raymond Hood, National Radiator Building (Ideal House), Great Marlborough Street, Westminster, 1927–9

Figure 13. Gordon Jeeves & H. O. Hamilton, Square House, Westminster, 1937–8

Figure 14. Collcutt & Hamp, New Adelphi, Adam Street, Westminster, 1936–8

Figure 15. Peter Behrens, New Ways, Northampton, 1925

bays. Now, under the influence of Heal's and Adelaide House, these are replaced by plain or almost plain stone posts.

Thus it is in Mr Sullivan's building for Courtauld's, Messrs Hobden & Porri's Britannia House, Shaftesbury Avenue, Mr Sullivan's excellent office building in Gracechurch Street, and an outstanding piece of proportioning – Messrs Richardson & Gill's office building in Wells Street.[3] Mr Markham in his Library Store for the British Museum [at Colindale] has, by translating the motif into brick architecture, given an unmistakably English and especially convincing character. In Lilley & Skinner's building in Oxford Street it is used only for the central portion of the front; in Drage's also in Oxford Street it is made more conspicuous by jazzy detail of the Paris 1925 type, and by the use of black granite, both these features having previously been tried out by the same architect in the National Radiator Building in Great Marlborough Street.[4] Amongst the most recent prominent examples of verticalism are Mr Hamp's Adelphi building and Messrs Jeeves and Hamilton's Berkeley Square House.[5]

PARIS 1925

The Paris Exhibition of 1925 can be regarded as the fountainhead of the Modern Movement in Britain. Several of the most opposed tendencies in architecture and decoration are to be traced back to it.

There is first the French Florid, a peculiar type of decoration which occurred in many of the French pavilions and had already before 1925 been used by René Lalique and also by the designers of fashionable Paris shop windows. It now appeared here and there in London, but its rather rich and sensuous appeal does not seem to have met with the approval of many British clients.

In the second phase, there is Jazz, that type of vulgar jagged ornament which swamped Britain immediately after the exhibition and did not lose its appeal until the beginning of the thirties. Even now it is still popular for cheaper rugs, electric fittings, fabrics and furniture.

Historically speaking, this nasty style of ornament has a complicated origin. It appears to be the outcome of German Expressionism, a serious revolutionary movement started about 1905 and rapidly spreading in the first post-war years. Sharp and spiky forms were then used to express revolt, the same feelings which made the French create Cubism. This violent and often brutal art entered e.g. into the figural work of the Bauhaus. While its serious meaning was kept here, it became soon lighter [and] more superficial when it was accepted into more commonplace domestic decoration. About 1922–23 objects of

3. L. Sylvester Sullivan: Courtaulds Warehouse, 16 St Martins Le Grand, 1924–5; 51–4 Gracechurch Street, 1928–30. Hobden & Porri, Britannia House, 233 Shaftesbury Avenue, 1929; Richardson and Gill, St Margaret's House, Wells Street, 1930–31.

4. Gordon Jeeves: Lilley & Skinner, 17–19 Oxford Street, 1931; Drage's, 73–89 Oxford Street, with H. A. Welch, 1929–30; National Radiator Building (Ideal House), with Raymond Hood, 1927–9.

5. Collcutt & Hamp, New Adelphi, Adam Street, 1936–8; Gordon Jeeves & H. O. Hamilton, Berkeley Square House, 1937–8.

Figure 16. Elisabeth Scott, Shakespeare Memorial Theatre, Stratford upon Avon, 1929–32

German Kunstgewerbe were covered with the characteristic forms of this popularised Expressionism. The 1923 exhibition at Munich was bristling with it. Swedish ornament of the same years looks very similar, and I have not yet been able to find out which way influences went.

It is obvious at any rate that there is only one step from this decorative manner to the international Jazz ornament. A further proof of the connections is the striking similarity of Paris details with some in Peter Behrens's house for Mr Bassett Lowke.[6] One may also compare ornament in the Gothenburg Exhibition of 1923 and the Austrian Pavilion in Paris in 1925.

The most noteworthy cases of something like Expressionism in English building decoration are to my mind Mr Kennington's brick figures on the façade of the Shakespeare Memorial Theatre. Particularly conspicuous instances of Jazz ornament on British soil are to be found in shops (some of Mr Emberton's above all), theatres and picture houses, some times with quite graceful, more often with hideous bastard shapes. As for the style of the more official French pavilions in Paris, this has made very little impression on this country. The only motif which may be related to it is the fluting of certain portions of façades, as it is now used quite frequently by architects over here.

Finally, there were in the Paris Exhibition also, of course, some highly revolutionary pieces of architecture by Le Corbusier, Mallet-Stevens, and the Russian architect Melnikoff [sic]. But these do not seem to have had an immediate effect upon Britain. The moment when this effect became noticeable marks the beginning of the Modern Movement in the narrower sense.

THE INTERNATIONAL MODERN MOVEMENT

Aesthetically speaking, the international Modern Movement is the synthesis of two apparently contradictory tendencies, the impermeability of the cube put up by human hands in opposition to nature, and the unhindered admission of nature outside into the inside of a building by means of a free fluctuation of air and light. Neither principle is new. The Palazzo Strozzi in Florence represents impermeability and human self-reliance in terms of the Italian Renaissance; the Palladian villa with its low wings and colonnades opening out into the surrounding scenery represents the opposite principle.[7] But never before our time has so far-reaching an attempt been made at combining the two principles.

The two principles may first be exemplified by two especially complete instances from abroad, Gropius's Bauhaus of 1925 and Le Corbusier's Pavillon de L'Esprit Nouveau at the Paris Exhibition of the same year.

6. Peter Behrens, New Ways, Northampton, 1925.

7. Giuliano da Sangallo, Cronaca and others, Palazzo Strozzi, Florence, 1489–1534.

The ground plan of the Bauhaus is totally asymmetrical; blocks of various shapes and heights are grouped together, so as to form a pattern that looks well and natural in the flat country around. But while so far as this goes that opposition to nature is avoided which classical symmetry always entails, there is no compromise with nature in the individual shapes themselves. No undulating outlines, no cornice, no roof. There are only strict verticals and horizontals such as never occur in nature. Walls are kept straight and unmitigated without plastic relief or convex and concave curves reminiscent of the lines of the human body. The windows are flush, and arranged in horizontal bands, in the precise rhythm of the abstract art of Moholy-Nagy or Mondrian. If in spite of all that the Bauhaus expresses a strong dramatic contrast, this is due to the juxtaposition of bare white walls completely consisting of glass.

Whether the introduction of the glass wall is regarded as representing the new century's enthusiasm for air, sun and out-door life, or its enthusiasm for technique, engineering and the conquest of matter by human genius – here is a sharp edge of a block suddenly made transparent, support withheld from a corner where support seems most necessary; here are cantilevered balconies with their metal railings that make you think of cruising, i.e. again of that typical combination of out-door enjoyment and machinery. In a combination of this kind precisely lay the unique importance of the Bauhaus as an art school: workshops and research laboratories to serve industry, and at the same time a centre of happy and adventurous community life.

Le Corbusier's Pavillon de l'Esprit Nouveau has also – though in a more lyrical way – something of this spirit of research coupled with a new openness of social life. For the small exhibition building was in fact put up to represent one unit out of a proposed block of six-storeyed flats. The closest symbolism with nature is aimed at. At the exhibition this ideal was demonstrated by the tree growing through the ceiling. The façade is boldly asymmetrical, with a full-height glass wall on the right, and a wide opening on the left giving access to various layers of inhabited space. The main living room behind the glass wall has again the same exciting freedom of spatial circulation. Part of this room is full height, another divided into two floors by a gallery. Even cupboards are on high steel legs so as to allow air to float beneath as well as above. All the details on the other hand are sharp and clear, made up from the simplest geometrical shapes, rectangular beams, circular posts, the little balcony a cube pure and simple – the same creative contrast of cubic and spatial elements as in the Bauhaus, although expressed by an artist of totally different character.

BRITAIN AND THE ART OF LE CORBUSIER

Architecture, this fact need not be repeated, is primarily the art of space, as sculpture is that of volume and painting that of the plane. Yet, except for a few cases during a few periods, the spatial arrangements of secular buildings have always consisted of a series of comparatively independent units, grouped so that their interrelation can be read out of the ground plan but not be taken in at one glance walking from one room to another. The 18th century for the first time in western civilisation conceived the ranges of rooms as spatial totalities. In Franconian and Austrian palaces of the Rococo the most fascinating compositions of staircase, *sala terrena* and main hall can be found. Charles Rennie Mackintosh again had a feeling for live space, and Frank Lloyd Wright went farther than anybody before him in establishing a spatial unity within the walls of a private house, but it was left to M. Le Corbusier – and in this I see his chief historic merit – to use the pretext of a house for creating a new conception of architectural space as an abstract art.

This is what chiefly impressed a number of architects in Britain since Le Corbusier's work first became known through publications and also through an exhibition stand which he did for Messrs Venesta Ltd in 1930.[8] In fact, the most brilliant achievements in the Corbusier spirit are exhibition work, i.e. jobs where the architect is freer as a creator than in ordinary domestic tasks. The MARS Exhibition of 1938 must be singled out, and above all Messrs Tecton's work for the zoos of London, Whipsnade and Dudley, unparalleled anywhere. The character of the Glasgow Exhibition buildings of 1938 was somewhat different, though also highly successful. Here one felt reminded now and then of that Scandinavian style ('Swedish B.') which characterised the Stockholm Exhibition of 1930 and later Swedish and Finnish exhibition pavilions, a style which would also hardly have evolved without the initial stimulus from Le Corbusier.

The rather uncomfortable airiness of Le Corbusier's ground plans, where no room is kept isolated from another, has only rarely inspired British architects – for reasons to be mentioned later. A unity of house and scenery on the other hand was bound strongly to appeal to the progressive amongst the English. Where they found it in illustrations of Le Corbusier's houses, or houses such as those which Gropius built for the Bauhaus staff, they must have responded to it immediately.

Similarly, in the case of factories, schools and hospitals and the like, the principle of free grouping as followed by Le Corbusier as well as Pre-Nazi Germany and the other Central European countries, has impressed architects over here. Amongst the most prominent examples of this principle are the pithead baths of the Miners' Welfare Committee. While one usually connects the international Modern Movement with buildings of a white monolithic appearance, some of the most recent pithead baths are built of bricks, and a number of the happiest experiments in free grouping in England have also been carried out in the traditional material. Even Mr Oliver Hill, in what seems to me the most brilliant of his domestic work, has now chosen brick to express that keen sense of spatial joy which goes through all his houses in whatever phantastic disguise it may have appeared in the past.[9] This reversion to brick is a tendency

8. Le Corbusier was commissioned in 1929 by Jack Pritchard to design a stand for Venesta at the Building Trades Exhibition the next year. Charlotte Perriand was in charge of the work. *Architects' Journal*, vol.72, 12 September 1930, p.445; Paolo Berdini, 'Le Corbusier in England: the Venesta Stand of 1929', in *AA Files*, no.15, Summer 1987, p.14.

9. Oliver Hill, Hill House, Redington Road, Hampstead, 1936–8.

Figure 17. C. G. Kemp, Snowdown Colliery, Kent, 1935

10. Lubetkin and Tecton, Highpoint II, Highgate, 1936–8.

11. Walter Gropius, 66 Old Church Street, Chelsea, 1935–6.

12. Maxwell Fry, Sun House, Frognal Way, Hampstead, 1934–5.

undeniable and reasonable. It is, as will be shown later, closely linked up with the growth of a specifically British Modern Movement.

Where foreign connections of such groups of brick buildings can be traced, they do not lead back to France but to Holland and the North of Germany. While this free grouping is a feature common to the modern style everywhere, there can be no doubt that the most boldly spatial elements to be found in this country or any other go back in some way to Le Corbusier.

Le Corbusier has put forward practical arguments for placing houses on concrete or steel posts leaving the ground-floor level open and unused. His main reason, however, is no doubt the aesthetic one to allow air to circulate beneath just as above. By raising a building in this manner it becomes disconnected from the soil, a lighter species of matter, as it were, no longer subject to the laws of gravity.

Whereas this motif expresses the successful attack of the outside atmosphere upon the foundations of the house, some other motif symbolises the free entrance of air into the walls.

Emphasis on the porch is one of Le Corbusier's favourite methods for achieving this. At Highpoint II, the concave curve of the porch slightly pointing forward towards the entrance clearly expresses the functional meaning of a liaison piece between outside and inside. In other English instances the shape of the porch rather indicates the transition from the fixed directions inside the building to the free rhythm of the surrounding nature.[10] Even in its simplest form – a boldly cantilevered slab of concrete sticking out over the door – it keeps its value as a token of space, a diving-board, as it were, which sends you off from the solid uprights of the building into the floating air around.

Treatment of the roof can be dictated by the same intentions. As it is often used for sun-bathing or otherwise made into inhabitable space, function and aesthetic expression go here clearly hand in hand. There may be a cantilevered concrete sun-roof on the roof, or there may just be a concrete girder to hand curtains from – the aesthetic value is the same, the formation of an intermediate zone between interior and exterior, another floor on which to live, and yet not a floor closed-in as the floors beneath. In Central Europe metal rods have often been used instead of the concrete beams. The effect is airier, and less material and also more of an engineering character than with Le Corbusier. And yet – this shows how intertwined relations are within the international Modern Movement – the first to introduce the French motif of the concrete roof girder and beam into London appears to have been Gropius in his Chelsea house.[11] However, in spite of such an anomaly, the fact remains that, generally speaking, Le Corbusier regards the volume of a building as something to be plastically shaped into the surrounding space, just as a sculptor of Cubism does, whereas Gropius regards it as the logical outcome of the technical and social considerations. Le Corbusier's genius is the artist's, Gropius's contains strong elements of the scientist's. Thus Corbusier's favourite material is concrete, Gropius's steel and glass. A comparison of the massive character of posts, balconies and roof in an English building is illustrated in this section with the lightness and grace of the same motifs in Mr Maxwell Fry's masterly house in Frognal Way, Hampstead, which shows clearly the difference between French and Central European treatment.[12]

The small concrete balconies which Le Corbusier has so often introduced are also less the outcome of practical than of aesthetic considerations – another attempt at transcending the borderline between within and without. Equally doubtful is the practical advisability, above all in this country, of uncovered outside staircases, but they too evidently express that open-air feeling which all buildings discussed in this group have in common.

Somewhat different is the reason for the popularity of another Corbusier motif, the port-hole. Greater than its pattern-value – the simple geometrical shape of the circle – is probably its associative value, the way in which it underlines the similarity of the modern house with its white walls, rounded corners, sweeping rows of windows, galleries and roof-terraces with the modern liner. The liner is in fact 'a machine to live in', as Le Corbusier wants the house of the 20th century to be.

Purely decorative, of no functional value, it seems, and therefore not popular with Le Corbusier is another French motif which was first noticed in M. Mallet-Stevens's Pavillón du Tourisme at the Paris Exhibition of 1925. I am referring to that odd crossing of the top-part of an upright by a few sharply projecting horizontals following each other closely. It is a strangely aggressive motif, typically 1920 in its violence and jazziness. It has infected the cinema style everywhere and also unfortunately found its way into many industrial products, such as electric fittings, hearth surrounds and the like. Its use in 'Tait's Tower' at the Glasgow Exhibition last year was understandable but, in my opinion, a pity because the prominent appearance of such a dated motif could easily detract the attention of visitors from the fact that most of the other buildings were of a far more progressive, logical and graceful character.[13]

PRE-NAZI GERMANY

French influence on contemporary British architecture is almost entirely confined to that of Le Corbusier, Mallet-Stevens and Lurçat, i.e. almost entirely to private houses. For only there can an architect, given appreciative clients, develop so much freedom as is necessary to put into architectural reality such gems of abstract art. A factory, an office building, a store, a school, a hospital, and a block of flats too, require as a rule so much more uniformity of general treatment that spatial play for its own sake is out of the question.

In these technically and socially more restricted tasks above all, the universalism of the new style becomes visible. A very limited number of motifs has proved sufficient to express, and express with a surprising amount of personal variety, what is needed. The resulting general uniformity and individual variation are both equally impressive and gratifying. The foremost country in evolving this style has been Germany in the fourteen years between the last war and the Nazi revolution. Precision and straightforwardness are the principal characteristics of this style. A scientific spirit pervades it. Its consistency, its usefulness, are opposed to Le Corbusier's licence. A purpose is stated, practical requirements are investigated, and the most direct formal expression of these is worked out.

The initial technical elements, at least for larger buildings, today are the steel or concrete girders or trusses. It would be dishonest to conceal this fact. Hence the initial aesthetic element of this style is the pure cube. Now you have your framework of verticals and horizontals, the inner walls can be inserted wherever you like them. Your outer walls are necessary only as a screen against rain and cold. There is consequently no reason for plastic moulding of a wall. What have you been commissioned to build? A factory? A maximum of light will probably be required. If you are dealing with more than one floor, your most logical way for providing this is to let your walls be of glass entirely. Gropius has had the courage in 1911 already to design a factory in this way. Britain, and for good national reasons, has only very rarely gone as far as that.

Or perhaps it is not quite logical after all to conceal the fact that there are several floors. Their existence should be expressed in the façades. Moreover, you may not want to kick your feet against glass while you are working near the outer wall. In that case you would interrupt your glass horizontally by bands of solid stone or concrete and brick. The most extreme rendering of this type, with alternating glass bands and solid bands right round a building of many

Figure 18. Thomas Tait, Tower of Empire, British Empire Exhibition, Glasgow, 1938

13. Thomas Tait, Tower of Empire, British Empire Exhibition, Glasgow, 1938 (demolished).

14. Mies van der Rohe, Reinforced Concrete Building, project 1922; Sir E. Owen Williams, D10 (Packed Wet Goods Factory), Boots, Beeston, Notts, 1931–2; Wallis, Gilbert and Partners, Electrical and Musical Industries (H.M.V.) Factory, Hayes, 1930 onwards; Adie, Button and Partners, Electroflo Factory, Park Royal, 1937; Joseph Emberton, Royal Corinthian Yacht Club, Burnham-on-Crouch, Essex, 1930; Louis de Soissons and Arthur Kenyon, Shredded Wheat Factory, Welwyn Garden City, 1925; Sir E. Owen Williams, Tunnel Cement Reinforced Concrete Laboratory, West Thurrock, Essex, 1932–3.

floors was a design of 1922 by Mies van der Rohe. It is followed by a few British buildings such as Sir Owen Williams' factory for Boots the Chemists of 1931/2, the H.M.V. Factory at Hayes, the Electroflo factory at Park Royal, in a freer particularly nautical-looking way with metal balconies by Mr Emberton at his Corinthian Yacht Club of 1930/31, on a smaller scale by Mr de Soissons in a factory in Welwyn, and for a building of one floor only by Sir Owen Williams in his Laboratories at Thurrock in Essex.[15] As a rule however, British architects seem to have disliked the bare logic and the naked appearance of such blocks. Some times they have tried superficially to cover this difficulty by introducing one more traditional motif, a grand entrance, or some jazzy detail. More often they have chosen another similar treatment, also of continental origin, but of a slightly less harsh character. For office-buildings above all another ratio of transparent and opaque wall will usually be required than for a factory. Not quite so much unmitigated light should be admitted. Individual windows would therefore be quite justifiable. The fact that they do not occur much more often in contemporary buildings can only be explained by referring once more to aesthetic reasons. The new style is always in favour of using a small number of large instead of using a large number of small motifs. Thus the system of alternating bands of wall and bands of window was almost bound to be created and developed. This development actually set in before the war. Vertical bands of wall and bands of window are distinguishing features of the Messel-motif, [while] horizontal bands were foreshadowed in houses of the Cottage-Style and Frank Lloyd Wright's houses, and more consistently used immediately after the last war. In a famous German example of 1927 the similarity with shipbuilding forms is again evident.[15]

The horizontal band of windows is the leitmotif for the majority of contemporary office buildings. No end of examples exist in practically all countries touched by the Modern Movement. The universal acceptance of this motif does not, however, mean an impoverishment. On the contrary. By agreeing to certain basic elements, a unity can at last be once more achieved similar to that which we know in the mediaeval town. Moreover, against such a background of satisfactory anonymity, the subtler achievements of architectural individuality stand out far more clearly than was possible in the late 19th century, an infinite variety of personal expression ranging from the pushing showiness of Mendelsohn's Herpich store in Berlin and [Kerr's] Commerce House, Middlesex Street, London, to the noble reserve of Salvisberg's travertine-faced Health Insurance Building in Berlin and Messrs Burnet, Tait & Lorne's Portland stone faced Steel House in Tothill Street, London.[16]

National differences are not so easily eliminated. On the continent, and in Germany above all, most of the outstanding examples of the horizontal scheme dispense as far as possible with posts setting the glass band into individual windows and keep the glass flush or nearly flush with the wall surface. Britain has as a rule disregarded this extremist solution and preferred to counterbalance the horizontal sweep by vertical posts at frequent intervals. Examples can be arranged according to varying proportions of window and posts. The more often posts are inserted, or the wider they are, the less revolutionary will be the appearance of the façade. This toning-down of the continental

15. This may be a reference to Walter Gropius's Auerbach house in Jena, or to the various buildings in Stuttgart's Weissenhofseidlung of that year.

16. Erich Mendelsohn, C. A. Herpich and Sons, Berlin, 1925 (demolished); H. Victor Kerr, Commerce House, Middlesex Street and Aldgate Avenue, 1932–4 (demolished); Otto R. Salvisberg, Deutsche Krankenversicherungs-AG, Berlin Schöneberg, 1929–30; Burnet, Tait and Lorne, Steel House, Tothill Street, Westminster, 1936.

Clockwise from left

Figure 22. Erich Mendelsohn, C. A. Herpich and Sons, Berlin, 1924

Figure 23. H. Victor Kerr, Commerce House, Middlesex Street and Aldgate Avenue, City of London, 1932–4

Figure 24. Burnet, Tait and Lorne, Steel House, Tothill Street, Westminster, 1936

motif may even go so far as the reintroduction within the horizontal bands of solid wall between individual windows. If the wall is furthermore of brick such as is to be found in Sir John Burnet, Tait & Lorne's Mount Royal Flats in Oxford Street, the final effect is unmistakably British.[17]

Two sub-species of the horizontal scheme must be added. It is sometimes used for buildings of only two storeys or even one, in which case it changes its expression considerably without, however, changing its essence. Two pairs of examples are illustrated to show the original continental as against the adapted British treatment.

Figure 25. Burnet, Tait and Lorne, Mount Royal Flats, Oxford Street, Westminster, 1933–4

Figure 26. William A. Johnson (with C. L. Paice and J. W. Cropper), C.W.S. Soapworks extension, Irlam, Greater Manchester, 1937–8

17. Burnet, Tait and Lorne, Mount Royal Flats (now Hotel), Oxford Street, Westminster, 1933–4.

18. Joseph Emberton, Simpson's, now Waterstone's, Piccadilly, Westminster, 1935–6; William A. Johnson (with C. L. Paice and J. W. Cropper), C.W.S. Soapworks extension, Irlam, Greater Manchester, 1937–8 (demolished).

19. H. S. Goodhart-Rendel, St Olave's House, Hay's Wharf, Southwark, 1931; P.L. Kramer, De Bijenkorf, Grote Marktstraat, The Hague, 1924–6.

20. E. Maxwell Fry and Elizabeth Denby, Kensal House, Ladbrooke Grove, Kensington, 1936.

Here are the instances in which decoration is applied to the horizontal scheme. Occasionally the window-posts get some horizontal lines, or if made of brick, an alternation of recessed and projecting bands. Occasionally, the window-band as a whole is framed. Occasionally, too, the solid bands are moulded. This is e.g. the case in Mr Emberton's building for Simpson's of Piccadilly. A more complicated treatment of window-bands has been used by Mr Johnson in his soap factory at Irlam. Each of them is divided by two long horizontal and frequent vertical concrete strips. The trellis effect thus created happens to be very similar to that of windows of a Dutch school near Amsterdam.[18]

Mr Goodhart-Rendel's Hay's Wharf of 1931 is a unique example. One may perhaps feel reminded, although in a very general way only, of the type of decoration which Piet Kramer used for the Bijenkorf Store at the Hague in 1926. One may also think of Swedish ornament, but both similarities are probably purely accidental.[19]

So much for horizontal schemes. Not always, however, can such a uniform fenestration be adopted. There are buildings, blocks of flats above all, where a more complex system of openings is required. Sometimes the case can simply be met by using individual windows instead of bands. Here the architect can either pretend that the horizontal scheme can yet be applied – this is done by over-emphasising the horizontal bands of solid, white wall between the windows – or he must think of another solution combining traditional fenestration with a contemporary effect. On the continent, some very successful blocks of flats exist, where the rhythm of differing spaced windows is the only motif that matters. In England only a very few can be found, by far the most prominent being Mr Maxwell Fry's Gas Company flats in Ladbroke Grove.[20]

Façades whose aesthetic value depends completely upon the harmonious proportion of individual windows in the walls are mainly to be seen in the less fanatic peripheral countries of Central Europe, Denmark, Scandinavia and Austria. England also possesses some. Sir John Burnet, Tait & Lorne's at Hackney may be singled out.[21]

A favourite motif for introducing some rhythm into an otherwise uniform façade is on the continent and in Britain to stress the contrast between the horizontals bringing together all rooms on the same floor level, and the necessary verticalism of the staircase. There is nothing new in this, and as long as a series of windows, one above the other, is used the motif cannot be regarded as illustrative of the principles of the Modern Movement. M. Perret in his house in rue Franklin in Paris in 1903 seems to have been the first to reduce the staircase wall to a huge sheet of glass, crossed only by bars of concrete. In this form, whether with transparent glass or glass bricks or a concrete trellis, it has become a stock motif of contemporary architecture.

While it emphasises height as against width, it does not give more than an indication of the third dimension extending behind the flush surface of the glass. The integrity of the front remains essentially untouched. In fact, the introduction of any plastic motifs to break this integrity is decidedly unusual today. You may find a projecting roof here and there, but it would be treated simply as a lid without a cornice linking it up with the wall. You may also find occasional window mouldings, but they would be only rectangular frames set hard against the wall and the opening. Thus Mr Hill has e.g. used them in his Morecambe Hotel and the joining café, and Messrs. Tecton in their group of small houses at Haywards Heath. In a very interesting way, incidentally, a similar kind of framing has been designed by Mr Lubetkin for a whole portion of the façade of Highpoint II, and for his four houses at Plumstead.[22]

To pass from such exceptional cases of a plastic treatment of facades to the more usual three-dimensional elements of architecture today, one difference between the continent and Britain must at once be stated. That desire for the visual expression of dashing speed which had made the unbroken white band so popular on the continent also led to whole facades being curved. This kind of streamlining, if the term may be applied here, characterises such buildings as Luckhardt & Anker's Telschow House, Peter Behrens's Tobacco Factory at Linz, Mendelsohn's Columbushaus, Brinkman & van der Vlugt's Tobacco Factory near Rotterdam and Pinguisson's hotel in St Tropez. Again Britain seems to deprecate such extremism. Peter Jones's in London, and Mr Haywood's Kennet House scheme in Manchester are almost the only comparable examples to be quoted.[23]

21. Probably a reference to Evelyn Court flats, Amherst Road, Hackney, 1934

22. Oliver Hill, Midland Hotel, Morecambe, Lancs, 1932–3; Lubetkin and Tecton, Sunnywood Drive, Haywards Heath, 1934–6; Lubetkin and Pilichowski, 85–91 (odd) Genesta Road, Plumstead, 1934–5.

23. Wassili and Hans Luckhardt and Alfons Anker, Telschow House, Berlin, 1926–8 (demolished); Peter Behrens (with Alexander Popp), State Tobacco Factory, Linz, Austria, 1929–38; Erich Mendelsohn, Columbushaus, Berlin, 1931; Brinkman and Van der Vlugt, Van Nelle Factory, Rotterdam, 1925–31; Georges-Henri Pingulisson, Hotel Latitude 43, St Tropez, 1931–2; William Crabtree, Slater and Moberly, Peter Jones, Chelsea, 1935–9; Leonard Haywood and R.A.H. Livett, Kennet House, Manchester, 1933–5 (demolished).

Figure 27. Burnet, Tait & Lorne, Evelyn Court, Hackney, 1934

Figure 28. Lennard Haywood and R. A. H. Livett, Kennet House, Cheetham, Manchester, 1933–35

24. D. Pleydell-Bouverie, shelter, shops
and funfair, Folkestone, 1937; Sir E. Owen
Williams, Pioneer Health Centre,
Peckham, 1935.

25. Fuller, Hall and Foulsham, Ibex
House, Minories, City of London, 1935–7;
Joseph Emberton, Universal House,
Southwark Bridge, 1933 (demolished
c.1960); Emil Fahrenkamp, Shellhaus,
Berlin-Tiegarten 1930–1; Viceroy Close,
Bristol Road, Birmingham, is in fact by
Mitchell and Bridgwater, Gollins and
Smeeton, from 1937.

Clockwise from left

Figure 29. Fuller, Hall and Foulsham,
Ibex House, Minories, City of London,
1935–7

Figure 30. Joseph Emberton, Universal
House, Southwark Bridge, 1933

Figure 31. Mitchell, Bridgewater,
Gollins & Smeeton, Viceroy Close,
Bristol Road, Birmingham, 1937

Another and, it seems, to British architects more acceptable method for
curving a façade is the introduction of a sequence of separate shallow bows,
obviously a much less violent method than that in use on the continent. Thus
it has been done in Mr Pleydell-Bouverie's gently undulating front of the
Folkestone Entertainments Pavilion, and, with quite a different expression of
energy and resilience, by Sir Owen Williams in his Peckham Health Centre.[24]

Otherwise, the only usual, and indeed an extremely usual, curve in British
façades of the Modern Movement is the rounded corner connecting two sides
of a rectangular building. The few cases where this motif is doubled or repeated more often than twice so as to result in what might be called [a] stag-
gered front are hardly worth mentioning. There is Messrs Fuller, Hall &
Foulsham's office building in the Minories, Mr Emberton's Universal House
for Beck & Pollitzer's and, strangely reminiscent of Fahrenkamp's Shell
Building [Berlin] in its general idea, Mr Yorke's Viceroy Court Flats in Birmingham.[25]

On the whole it can safely be said that spatial movement is not what British architects wish to express in their buildings. It is highly characteristic in
this connection that the only English town hall of a strictly Modern Movement
character, Mr Culpin's new Poplar Town Hall, incorporates the usual motif of
the rounded corner with horizontal bands, but stops the flow of the
horizontals by the insertion of a centre block at the corner with a tall shallow
bay-window. Very hesitant is also the treatment of a similar motif in Mr
Cameron Kirby's excellent filling station at Staines. This little piece of architecture incidentally is surprisingly reminiscent in its general layout of
Mendelsohn's Metal Workers' Trade Union Building in Berlin, a building
completed slightly later than Mr Kirby's.[26]

Where the third dimension plays an important part in British facades, it is as a rule confined to one particular motif and does not penetrate the whole of the composition. The staircase is an especially frequent medium. It can be hidden behind a vertical row of low windows with the rest of the front recessed or projecting, as has been done very successfully in Messrs H. Tanner's warehouse for Boots.[27] Or it can be put into a slightly projecting tower, the most usual arrangement in German pre-Nazi flats. Or else the row of windows in the staircase tower can be replaced by one tall window. As a rule this is flanked by solid walls, but every now and then the whole front of the staircase tower is reduced to a glass sheet. Thus Mr Lubetkin has done it in Highpoint II, creating a maximum spatial thrill out of a simple motif in its relation to other equally simple motifs surrounding it. The staircase at the Mount Royal Flats is constructionally similar but quite different in expression. By keeping the glass front very narrow and providing it with an odd tapering base, the architects have given the motif a surprisingly traditional, as it were bay-window appearance.

A treatment which is sometimes particularly effective is the placing of the glass parts of a staircase tower across the corner. There is more stimulus in this for appreciating the motif spatially than in the flat glass front. The fullest spatial value, however, can only be derived from the staircase if it is completely surrounded by glass. Only [with] this a full unity is reached between the smooth surface of the front and the movements in space going on inside. Gropius is to be considered the creator of this motif. In his factory at the Cologne Exhibition of 1914 he has put the staircase, as it were, into a test tube. We see the coiled apparatus inside as though the steps and railings were a piece of mechanised art by Moholy-Nagy or Gabo. The synthesis of impermeability and transparency here achieved is of ideal purity.[28] In this country, Messrs. Mendelsohn and Chermayeff have repeated the motif in their Bexhill Pavilion, adding circular galleries to the outside. Mendelsohn in the Stuttgart Schocken Store had years before adapted the same motif to a straight façade where no corner was available for it. It is here and in one or two British derivations from it combined with the horizontal scheme.

Other German architects endeavoured to obtain an effect of lucidity similar to that of Gropius's factory by putting the staircases into rectangular boxes. This again has once or twice also been done by architects in this country. But there is evidently on the whole a tendency over here not to go too far, and rather to keep a circular or rectangular staircase tower closed by solid walls, or at least to solidify it by the introduction of stone of concrete uprights between the glass panels.

Figure 32. Stuart Cameron Kirby, Service Station for Stewart and Ardern, Staines, 1934

Figure 33. Clifford Culpin (E. G. Culpin and Son), Poplar Town Hall, Bow, 1937–8

26. Clifford Culpin, (E. G. Culpin and Son), Poplar Town Hall, Bow, 1937–8 (part demolished 2000); Stuart Cameron Kirby, Service Station for Stewart and Ardern, Staines, 1934; Erich Mendelsohn, Administration Building, Metal Workers' Union, Berlin, 1929.

27. Henry Tanner (E. T. Dowling and W. H. Tanner), Canteen, Recreation Building and Day Continuation School (not a warehouse), Beeston, Notts, 1938.

28. Walter Gropius, Office Building and Maclure Hall, Werkbund Exhibition, Cologne, 1914.

Loggias and galleries, above all in blocks of flats, are two more motifs that can be given as much or as little spatial value as the individual architect wants. They can be bound tightly into the façade by means of horizontal bands, or else they can be used to destroy the solid appearance of the wall, frequently in conjunction with staircase towers or bay windows made entirely or mainly of glass, or with corner windows. Any effect, from the most delicate to the most dramatic, is possible. To illustrate this wide range of expression obtainable despite the limited number of motifs, Mr Wells Coates's Lawn Road Flats of 1934 may be compared with Mr Maxwell Fry's second block of flats in Ladbroke Grove (1938).[29] The two motifs to which both compositions are confined are galleries in front of four floors, and a tall staircase window against which the galleries run at right angles. The contrast between cyclopic weight in the one [and] immaterial lightness in the other building is most telling. It can be recognised especially clearly at the points where the galleries meet the wall in front of the staircase.

One more three-dimensional element only must be mentioned, because it is a favourite with British architects. Others space does not allow to discuss. I am referring to the semi circular bay which is used either one-storeyed with a solid wall and a window only towards one side, or with a window-band right round, or constructed entirely of glass. It can also be found two storeys high, with only a low window-band near the bottom, or with a larger expanse of glass. In the case of the Berlei Factory, one of Britain's best small factories, the upper part of the bay is built of glass bricks, and the juxtaposition of the bay against a long two-storeyed façade of the horizontal scheme is superb.[30]

In some of the most pleasant of London's flats the semi-circular bay is taken up right through four or more floors, to replace, as it were, the polygonal Victorian bay window. Mr Atkinson's Stockleigh Hall and Regency Lodge are perhaps the finest examples of this type. The motif as such is, incidentally, not new at all, nor is it new in this particular form, but, as Mr Atkinson incorporates it into his compositions, it becomes an integral part of a whole so entirely English that it could never be mistaken for anything else. Here then is an example of present-day architecture both contemporary and British in character.[31]

TOWARDS A BRITISH MODERN MOVEMENT

The argument is sometimes heard (and it will probably be heard more often in the near future) that the Modern Movement is essentially un-English in spirit. This may seem true at first sight, but in a deeper sense it is not. There is certainly no denying the fact that some of its most brilliant achievements in this country are the work of architects of foreign origin and training. There is, however, nothing fundamentally wrong with that. It can afford even today to be offering hospitality to, and receiving inspiration from, architects of many na-

29. Wells Coates, Lawn Road Flats (Isokon Building), Belsize Park, 1932–4; Maxwell Fry, 65 Ladbroke Grove, 1938.

30. Sir John Brown and A. E. Henson with W. David Hartley, Berlei Corset Factory, Slough, 1937.

31. Robert Atkinson and A. F. B. Anderson, Stockleigh Hall, Prince Albert Road, Regent's Park, 1936–7; Regency Lodge, Swiss Cottage, 1935–7.

Figure 34. Sir John Brown & Henson, Berlei Factory, Slough, 1937

Figure 35. Robert Atkinson and A. F. B. Anderson, Stockleigh Hall, Prince Albert Road, Regent's Park, 1936–7

tionalities, just as the Paris school of painting and sculpture is composed of elements from everywhere. What would be disastrous is only if England, the land of the strongest traditions and the strongest common sense, proved unable to absorb that outside inspiration so amply provided for her. This, however, is not the case.

It is my intention in this last section to show that a British Modern Movement is possible, and in fact exists. For one thing, there is nothing un-English in the individual elements of the new style. Where the French mediaeval cathedral is a ravishing spatial unity, the English is a complex group of separate blocks (two transepts, not one!) screened off from each other, or actually divided by walls, as in Anglo-Saxon churches. Rectangular choirs and Lady-chapels are an English feature, while they are as a rule semi-circular or polygonal on the continent.

When the Gothic style became nationally differentiated, France developed her Flamboyant, Germany her spatial and over-decorated Late-Gothic, Italy her Renaissance in Gothic disguise, but England created Perpendicular, a style as intensely English as anything can be, and a style based entirely on hard uprights and horizontals.

Again, when the so-called Northern Renaissance spread everywhere, the English soon abandoned the international (originally Netherlandish) idiom of the day, and evolved a version of their own in which decoration is confined to a few places such as gables, whereas the walls are left bare and widely opened by rectangular windows as large as today. The same spirit led the English to substitute Palladianism for Baroque. It accounts for the fact that this country has not produced one of Europe's greatest sculptors. It culminated in the architecture of the London brick house of the late 17th and 18th centuries. Here are plain flush walls, well proportioned unmoulded windows, adornment rigidly restricted to the entrance and its surround. And here is uniformity to an extent never reached again before the Modern Movement.

Besides such general architectural principles, there are also certain individual motifs of British period styles which closely resemble contemporary motifs, e.g. the segmental or semi-circular bay of the Regency or the way in which light metal balconies and galleries were placed like transparent screens around such bays or in front of façades of the same date. But the general principles are of course more important. And since simplicity, uniformity, rectangularity, abrogation of ornament have been specifically English in the past, a movement dependent so much on these cannot be un-English as such.

What is un-English in both Le Corbusier and Gropius is their fanaticism, whether social or aesthetic. In the work of the continental leaders of the Modern Movement, no trace of tradition is left. Abolishing every single form from the past was the first thing the progressive German, French and American architects did before the last war, when they took over the new ideas from Britain.

In Britain, in the meantime, two new and extremely pleasant compromises between old and new were found. Mr Voysey's Cottage Style and Sir Ernest Newton's Neo-Georgian. Both grew rapidly, at first independent of each other, but soon so closely intertwined that it is often impossible to say to which of the two traditionalist tendencies a building belongs. To this revised traditionalism are due some of the best houses designed in England between 1920 and 1925. Some of them have been illustrated before. A few more recent ones may now be added, Mr Milne's Northfields School at Dunstable, where in a very appealing way the simple horizontal windows of the Cottage Style are combined with the hipped roof and the lantern turret of Neo-Georgian, Mr Fletcher's Children's Home at [Smethwick], again a successful combination of motifs from both sources.[32] Mr Topham Forrest's flats for the London County Council which one can hardly call Neo-Georgian or anything but truly contemporary, although any demonstrative breach with tradition is carefully avoided. The

32. Oswald Milne, Northfields School, Dunstable, 1935 (demolished); Roland Fletcher and Chester Button, Children's Home at Smethwick, Birmingham, 1938.

same constructive attitude characterises Mr de Soissons's work, and Mr James's or Mr Atkinson's.

As for Mr Atkinson, his Wallington Town Hall provides an exceptional case. Here a general atmosphere of tradition is kept in spite of details which are all clearly of the 20th century.[33] Exactly the reverse of this has been Mr Newton's method when he added to the Neo-Georgian Memorial Hall at Marlborough College the new Science Block in 1933. He accomplished what may seem impossible, the satisfactory combination of a star-shaped group of laboratories with uncovered concrete walls and large horizontal windows – as unmitigated as anything Sir Owen Williams has built – with a dainty little Swedish or Georgian lantern of sympathetic design.[34]

Clockwise from left

Figure 36. Roland Fletcher and Chester Button, Children's Home at Smethwick, Birmingham, 1938.

Figure 37. London County Council (G. Topham Forrest, Chief Architect), Springfield Estate, Wandsworth Road, Lambeth, 1935

Figure 38. Robert Atkinson, Town Hall for Beddington and Wallington UDC, Wallington, 1933–5

Figure 40. Herbert Welch and F. M. Lander, The Ridings, Hanger Hill Estate, Ealing, 1934

Figure 39. W. G. Newton, Memorial Hall and Science Building, Marlborough College, 1933

Amongst buildings combining individual modern and individual traditional motifs in such a way as to attain effects of unity in the end, there are also a few – too few unfortunately – suburban housing estates of small semi-detached houses. Mr Welch, e.g. in one of these which is illustrated here, has introduced the large horizontal windows and rounded corners of the Modern Movement into a composition of essentially traditional appearance. While certainly houses of this type must be regarded as the principal starting-off point for a British Modern Movement, it would be wrong to assume that there are no British architects of strong personality who have contributed new and independent solutions to the international modern style. There are several – just as there are certain modern themes specially developed or even created in England, e.g. the planned trading estate, the pithead bath or the health centre. One of the most outstanding of the independent British leaders of the Modern Movement in the international sense is Sir Owen Williams. With the engineer's directness of approach and an enthusiasm for concrete similar in intensity to that of the great Frenchmen Perret and Garnier, he has, in his first factory for Boots with its large glass surfaces divided only by thin white lines and chamfered at the corners, his Empire Pool at Wembley with its enormous concrete fins, his flats at Stanmore so logical and straightforward as on the continent only Max Taut has been, and with his second factory for Boots with its immensely cantilevered loading dock, created monuments of international significance. His name is also connected with another of the most prominent

British modern buildings, Messrs. Ellis & Clarke's Daily Express of 1932, where the continental conception of the glass façade is treated boldly and to a certain degree independently, the leading idea being a new combination of the horizontal scheme and the complete glass block with a rounded corner by means of alternating bands of transparent and black glass.[35]

Perhaps the most instructive case of a British treatment of an international theme is Peter Jones's store in Sloane Square by Messrs Slater & Moberly, Professor Reilly and Mr Crabtree. A happy balance is here reached between the extreme horizontalism of the one and the extreme verticalism of the other favourite continenal store scheme. The thin but frequent vertical lines stop the horizontal flow of the glass bends along the gently curved façade. In Mr Wells Coates's Embassy Court at Brighton a similar interaction of the two dimensions is presented, resulting in a calm yet vigorous balance.

Now this balance is precisely the quality by which the British – subconsciously as a rule, one may presume – try to widen the range of expression accessible to modern architecture. They are not entirely alone in their endeavour. Some few Dutch and Northern German architects (above all Fritz Schumacher of Hamburg, one of the wisest of German architects and townplanners and consequently dismissed in 1933) have been working in a very similar spirit.

To illustrate the specifically British approach to the Modern Movement in some of its implications, I have chosen twenty examples.

One way to make balance visible is symmetry, although not necessarily the rigid symmetry of classic canons. By building up a façade symmetrically in the main, one of the most significant elements of restlessness in continental architecture is at once removed. Symmetrical are Mr Atkinson's flats such as Stockleigh Hall, Mr James's Slough Urban District Offices, the new libraries at Swansea by Mr Rees and the smaller especially charming one at Norris Green, Liverpool by Mr Keay, symmetrical is the Morecambe Hotel and Mr Musman's Comet Inn at Hatfield, easily the best designed pub in Britain.[36]

A looser balance without strict symmetry characterises such private houses as Mr R. D. Russell's at Colwall, Mr Guy Morgan's at Twyford, and Miss Crowley's at Cambridge.[37] In Mr Russell's house small upright windows on the left are separated from large wide windows on the right by a spacious semicircular bay. The result is quiet harmony. If anywhere, Mr Voysey might here give his blessing to the Modern Movement, which is a great compliment. Another compositional element to obtain balance in spite of avoiding identical motifs is the juxtaposition of windows of different proportion on the different floors of a building. Where continental architects would have enjoyed the hard monotony of twice repeated horizontal bands of the same size, Professor Reilly in his buildings for the Liverpool School of Architecture carefully differentiates between the static ground floor windows and the sweep of the lower band above.[38] Messrs Stanley Hall and Easton & Robertson in the Metropolitan Water Board Laboratories have designed a deeply satisfactory group of a concave mainly horizontal wing and a convex mainly vertical block at one end. While this part has finely shaped tall upright windows only, the long wing on the left has two bands of windows of which however only the top one runs through uninterruptedly. The ground floor windows are upright and boldly framed.[39]

Reversely, in Mr Rees's library the bottom windows are strictly horizontal, but the ones in the upper block are predominantly vertical. The composition of the recessed parts of Mr James's Slough Urban District Council Offices can also be compared, and even – as has been pointed out before – such international-looking buildings as Peter Jones's. It may be added that an apparently so much less progressive front as that of Mr Marwick's temporary offices for the Bank of Scotland in Edinburgh is in fact also representative of the same tendency. There are here again the thin uprights to counter-balance the win-

33. Robert Atkinson, Town Hall for Beddington and Wallington UDC, 1933–5.

34. W. G. Newton, Memorial Hall, Marlborough College, Wiltshire, 1925; Laboratories 1933.

35. Sir E. Owen Williams: Boots D10; Empire Pool (now Wembley Arena), Wembley, 1933–4; Flats, Dennis Lane and Valencia Road, Stanmore, 1933–6 (reclad); Boots D6 (Packed Dry Goods Factory), Beeston, Notts, 1935–8; Daily Express, Fleet Street, City, 1929–31.

36. C. H. James and Bywaters and Rowland Pierce, Slough Town Hall, 1934–6; Verner O. Rees, Main Library, University College, Swansea, 1935–7; Lancelot H. Keay (City Architect's Department), Harry A. Cole Library, Norris Green, Liverpool, 1937; Oliver Hill, Midland Hotel, Morecambe, 1932–3; E. B. Musman, Comet Inn, Hatfield, Herts, 1933.

37. R. D. Russell and Marian Pepler, Lobden, Upper Colwall, near Malvern, 1932; Guy Morgan, Land's End House, Twyford, Berks, 1934–5; Mary Crowley, three houses for family and friends at Tewin, Herts (not Cambridge), 1936.

38. Reilly, Budden and Marshall, School of Architecture and Building Engineering, Liverpool, 1933.

39. John Murray Easton of Easton and Robertson, Laboratory Building (now flats), Metropolitan Water Board, New River Head, Islington, 1938.

Above · top row · left to right

Figure 41. Sir Owen Williams, Flats in Valencia Road, Stamore, Middlesex, 1936

Figure 42. C. H. James & Bywaters and Rowland Pierce, Slough Town Hall, 1934–6

Figure 43. Lancelot H. Keay, Harry A.Cole Library, Norris Green, Liverpool, 1937

Above · bottom row · left to right

Figure 43. E. B. Musman, Comet Hotel, Hatfield, 1935

Figure 44. R. D. Russell & Marian Pepler, Lobden, Colwall, Hereford & Worcester, 1932

Figure 45. C. H. Reilly, L. B. Budden & J. E. Marshall, Liverpool School of Architecture, 1933

Below · clockwise from left

Figure 46. John Murray Easton of Easton and Robertson, Laboratory Building, Metropolitan Water Board, New River Head, Islington, 1938

Figure 47. Sir Giles Gilbert Scott, Guinness Brewery, Park Royal, 1933–5 (demolished)

Figure 48. Oliver Hill, Hill House, Redington Road, Hampstead, 1937

Figure 50. T. P. Marwick, National Bank of Scotland, temporary head office, George Street,Edinburgh, 1936

Figure 49. Ernst Freud, 1–6 Frognal Close, Hampstead, 1937

dow bands, and the faintly pointed panels in between also prevent the looker-on from reading the façade horizontally.[40] And why does Mr Oliver Hill in his Morecambe Hotel introduce framed windows between the horizontal bands and solid white posts between the glass panels of the centre staircase, if not for holding up movements of the greater violence? [sic] Or why does he, in his most recent, and in my opinion, most masterly private house, the one in Redington Road, Hampstead, oppose the verticalism of the loggia to the general horizontalism of the rest of the block? For reasons connected with the sloping site? Certainly, but what he has made of it is another especially brilliant proof of the potentialities usually still hidden of a genuinely British Modern Movement. Compare this house, motif after motif, inside and outside, with, say, Mies van der Rohe's famous Tugendhat House in Brno, and you have, convincingly to anybody, I think, who has a feeling for architectural expression, the proof of what profound and constructive differences are possible within the same universal modern style.

One significant fact about all the houses illustrated in this group is that they are built of brick. There is in this reversion to a traditional material again something typically British. Why are the most British looking factories, Sir Giles Gilbert Scott's Guinness Brewery at Park Royal and his Battersea Power Station, brick buildings? Why is brick the material of the excellent small factories on the

40 Thomas P. Marwick and Son, Temporary Head Offices, National Bank of Scotland, George Street, Edinburgh, 1935–6.

41. Sir Giles Gilbert Scott, Guinness Brewery, Park Royal, Ealing, 1933–5 (demolished); Battersea Power Station, 1930–5, 1944–55; W. G. Holford (master plan and core buildings), Team Valley Trading Estate, Gateshead, 1937–.

42. Ernö Goldfinger, 1–3 Willow Road, Hampstead, 1937–9; Ernst Freud, 1–6 Frognal Close, Hampstead, 1937.

Team Valley Trading Estate?[41] Why has even Mr Lubetkin used brick at Highpoint II (although in almost as sophisticated a way as he used the Erecthaeum figures), and Messrs Tecton in their group of small houses at Hayward's Heath, and Mr Goldfinger in his house at the bottom of Downshire Hill, Hampstead, and Mr Freud in his houses in Frognal?[42] Obviously, brick must have something extremely appealing and convincing for the English atmosphere, if it could attract these foreign architects working in London.

The London Passenger Transport Board was amongst the patrons of architecture in London to decide in favour of brick, after having commissioned its first modern stations before 1932 in concrete. The series of brick-built stations on the Piccadilly Line, mainly designed and erected in 1932 and 1933, are the work of Messrs Adams, Holden & Pearson, Mr C. H. James and Mr Heaps. They are among the highest achievements of modern British architecture, the best buildings of their kind in Europe and worthy to be placed side by side with the best of the London brick houses of about 1700. The variety with which Mr Holden has treated the same task is admirable. In some stations the reception

Figure 51. Adams, Holden and Pearson, Wood Green Underground Station, 1931–2

Figure 52. Adams, Holden and Pearson, Arnos Grove Underground Station, 1932

Figure 55. Stanley Hall, Easton and Robertson, Oxford University Press Warehouse, Neasden, 1929–30 (demolished)

Figure 56. Joseph Emberton, Olympia, Kensington, 1929

Figure 57. Burnet, Tait and Lorne, Curzon cinema, Mayfair, 1933

43. Charles Holden: Enfield West (with C. H. James, now Oakwood Station) 1932–3; Wood Green, 1931–2; Chiswick Park, 1932; Arnos Grove, 1932.

hall is combined with a tower, in others with a range of shops, and the reception halls themselves present an infinite variety of subtle modifications. It is worth comparing in detail the rectangles of Enfield West and Wood Green, or the cylinders of Chiswick Park and Arnos Grove.[43] At Chiswick Park there are, as will be noticed, low and heavy square pillars on the ground floor and a light drum with large glass surfaces above, while Arnos Grove has a glass-faced angular bottom block and a more closed and solid looking centre drum. These stations, and most of the other buildings illustrated in this last section are practical without any modern engineering romanticism, dignified but not overbearing – in short British in every respect and as immediately convincing as an accumulation of the best British qualities can make them.

A NOTE ON HOLLAND

In Holland, the Modern Movement appeared in two different forms, one international and one national. The international was represented by Oud, Stam and some others, the national first of all by the so-called Phantasts. These worked as a rule in brick and indulged in a type of wild and outré decoration derived from Dutch Art Nouveau, Berlage, the Dutch East Indies and Frank Lloyd Wright. The Amsterdam housing schemes which owing to their large scale planning became famous all over Europe, have roofs of unexpected bulging shapes, balconies and galleries placed irregularly and windows of assorted forms. Schools, etc., such as those by Dudok, also avoid symmetry. Unpierced brick walls alternate with walls decorated by bands of exceedingly low windows. Around entrances, brick ornament of cubistic character is often found.

British connections with Holland are not frequent. Those with the style of Oud and van der Vlugt can hardly be traced accurately, because they merge into the international Modern Movement in general. As to the more specifically Dutch style, Mr Emberton may have remembered the heavy irregular forms of the Phantasts when he designed the outside and inside of Olympia; and Messrs John Burnet, Tait and Lorne seem to have expressed their appreciation of the lighter type of Dutch brick decoration in details of the Masonic Hospital and the Curzon Cinema. As to the pleasant Dutch grouping of low brick blocks which most people over here would link up with the name of Dudok, this may have inspired British architects more frequently than can actually be shown. To mention just one case I could imagine Mr Howard Robertson's warehouse for the Oxford University Press which was erected as early as 1929/30 to be influenced to a certain extent by Dudok, on whose work Mr Robertson had written in the *Architectural Review* in 1923. More instances of a similar nature could be enumerated, if space allowed to do so.

2 MODERNISM AND TRADITION IN ENGLISH SCULPTURE 1929–39

CHRIS STEPHENS

MODERNISM AND TRADITION IN ENGLISH SCULPTURE 1929–39

CHRIS STEPHENS

This paper is something of an introduction to some of the issues around sculpture in the late 1920s and the 1930s. Some of these, specifically the relationships between modernist art and an English vernacular, have been aired by me in another context.[1] It is nevertheless apposite to bring them within the rubric of a consideration of a national modernism. The present essay is principally about the sculpture of Barbara Hepworth, but will also consider the work of other sculptors, and the issues raised may be seen to apply to a wider sculptural production. I shall be looking largely at the theories which informed Hepworth's work in the earlier part of our decade with the intention to extend these forward to her later work. In the process, I shall position her and the work in relation to other cultural producers in Britain. Underlying this treatment are one or two broader questions.

First, I am struck by the persistent association of modernist art with architecture and design in studies of this period. That is to say, to stage an exhibition of 1930s design one is expected, it seems, to include the painted and sculpted works of Ben Nicholson, Barbara Hepworth, Henry Moore, Paul Nash and others in a way that one would not have to in a presentation of design of the 1940s, say, or the 1970s. This association was highlighted by the inclusion of a Surrealist section in the 'Modern Britain' exhibition. For surrealism I would say, it is less easy to claim a cohesive co-operation between fine artists and designers. This reveals the reiteration of the perception of modernism in Britain in the mid-and late 1930s as a binary opposition between Surrealism and Constructivism. Of course, the exhibition is full of examples of the intervention of artists in the design of domestic fabrics or in advertising but, whether these resulted from economic expediency on the part of the artist, or from a belief – derived from the Bauhaus – in collaboration between artists and designers, art and industry, this persistent duality is symptomatic of a certain, narrow understanding of modernism as defined by formalism and internationalism.

In looking at the work of Hepworth and her associates, I want to consider what it was that defined her sculpture as modern and to extrapolate from that a more complex, less monolithic idea of modernism. Specifically, I want to question the perception that national tradition and modernism are, by definition, opposed to each other. This question informed much of the art of the period and was articulated within the critical discourse around it. Similarly, it continually re-emerges within historical analyses: in 1932 Paul Nash considered whether 'Going Modern and Being British' was a feasible proposition, and later in the decade a range of articles on aspects of English culture appeared in modernist contexts, such as the magazine *Axis* and Myfanwy Piper's anthology *The Painter's Object* (1937).[2] Charles Harrison's *English Art and Modernism* (1981) can be said to be predicated on the perceived opposition of insularity and modernism, and some of the conjunctions of the two categories are set out in Judy Collins's essay in the 'Modern Britain' catalogue. The nature of the relationship between Englishness and modernism has recently been debated

Figure 1. Hepworth *Figure of a Woman* 1929–30, Corzehill Stone, Tate (Hepworth Estate)

1. See my 'Ben Nicholson: Modernism, Craft and the English Vernacular' in David Peters Corbett, Ysanne Holt and Fiona Russell, eds., *The Geographies of English Art: Landscape and the National Past in English Art 1880–1940*, New Haven and London, Yale University Press.

2. Paul Nash, 'Going Modern and Being British', *Weekend Review*, March 1932.

and problematised but I feel that there still persists a simplistic idea that indigenous material is by definition anathema to ideas of the modern and that this idea is itself often based upon unquestioning notions of what is 'English' – the landscape, for example.

The radicalism of the art of the 1930s has been reinforced, if not actually defined in part, by the perception of the 1940s as a period of nationalistic reaction. Harrison saw *The Painter's Object* – which carried two essays by John Piper, one on 'Early English Art' and the other, a recall to artistic order, 'Lost a Valuable Object' – as symptomatic of 'the growth of an insular and conservative tendency' in the later 1930s.[3] Such symptoms have repeatedly been presented as constituting a reactionary retreat into a cultural production that sought links to national traditions in preference to modernist internationalism. In 1972 Alan Bowness observed that for a long time the 1940s had been

> *a dark decade of British art – sandwiched between the pioneering thirties when a fresh and positive internationalism swept into British art, and the fifties when so many of today's artists and attitudes were formed.*[4]

The 1940s, he went on, were usually considered 'best forgotten ... a depressed area, when art came to a halt and the new talent that emerged trailed off in unrewarding directions'. Even in the context of this early attempt to rehabilitate the painting of the 1940s, the best claim that Bowness could set against such criticism was that the work 'now begins to take on a certain remoteness and a period charm'. Since then, of course, a new, pluralistic, post-modern art history has found obscured values and points of interest in the art of the 1940s. Nevertheless, the perception of a nationalistic reaction to an internationalistic modernism persists. In considering Barbara Hepworth between 1929 and 1939,

3. Charles Harrison, *English Art and Modernism*, London: Allen Lane and Bloomington, Indiana: Indiana University Press, 1981, pp.321–2.

4. Alan Bowness, 'Introduction', *Decade 40s*, Arts Council tour, 1972–3, p.5.

Figure 2. Hepworth's studio, Hampstead, 1933 (Hepworth Estate)

I would hope to suggest that what constituted the modern in art (and in architecture and design) was more diverse and nuanced than this binary model will allow, and so to challenge the perceived, necessary opposition of Englishness and modernism.

The nature of the work which Hepworth was producing at the beginning of our period, in 1929, was formulated earlier in the 1920s. With her husband, John Skeaping, and Henry Moore, she was seen as one of the leading figures of the 'new movement' in sculpture, which was characterised by its adherence to the twin doctrines of 'direct carving' and 'truth to materials'. Other artists who might have qualified for the same label included Maurice Lambert, Alan Durst, Richard Bedford, Gertrude Hermes, Betty Muntz and Leon Underwood. The elevated importance of the artist's actual carving of the final work of art, as opposed to his or her modelling of a maquette to be translated by craftsmen, and the belief in the determination of the work's form by its material, had been established as key elements of modern sculpture, in Britain and abroad, at an earlier moment. They had been pioneered in Britain by Eric Gill, Jacob Epstein and Henri Gaudier-Brzeszka before the First World War, and Constantin Brancusi and Amadeo Modigliani were their most renowned Parisian advocates. In 1924 Gill advocated sculptures 'which owe part of their quality to the material of which they are made and of which the material inspires the workman and is freely accepted by him'.[5] Hepworth was taught to carve in 1925 by the Italian *marmista* (marble blocker) Giovanni Ardini, through the mediation of Skeaping, and in her first public statement in 1930, she clearly aligned herself with Gill's position:

> *Carving to me is more interesting than modelling because there is an unlimited variety of materials from which to draw inspiration. Each material demands a particular treatment and there are an infinite number of subjects in life each to be re-created in a particular material. In fact, it would be possible to carve the same subject in a different stone each time, throughout life, without a repetition of form.*[6]

Moore would articulate the same position a few weeks later when he wrote that the sculptor had been

> *freed ... to recognise again the importance of the material in which he works, to think and create in his material by carving direct, understanding and being in sympathy with his material so that he does not force it beyond its natural constructive build.*[7]

The rather staged photograph of Hepworth's studio in 1933, showing a number of unfinished carvings, an array of tools – chisels, rasps, hammers – spread across the table and a large block of uncarved rock ready to be tackled, reiterates the importance and the labour of the process of carving.

Thus Hepworth and her circle were perceived as the inheritors of a recent tradition, their position facilitated by the battles endured by their predecessors and Epstein in particular. Indeed, the 'new movement' in sculpture was presented by one critic as a relaxation of the 'scholasticism' of earlier modernist art. Writing in November 1930, to coincide with Hepworth and Skeaping's joint exhibition at Tooth's gallery, John Grierson noted that 'having stripped in good Carlylean fashion the body of sculpture of all representational, literary, and other furbelows – [sculpture] begins to develop a certain looseness of limb' and the sculptors were seen to 'have no obligation to be so desperately and laboriously Evangelical'.[8]

Conscious of their debt, it would seem, the younger artists paid their respects to the sculptors and theorists of the earlier generation and cited common sources of inspiration. Specifically, they followed Epstein's arder, and the theorists of Bloomsbury – Roger Fry and Clive Bell – in admiring the three-dimensional works of non-Western cultures. Moore would recall as a personal epiphany his encounter with Roger Fry's collection of essays *Vision and Design*

5. Eric Gill, *Sculpture: An Essay on Stone-cutting with a preface about God*, Ditchling, 1924.

6. Barbara Hepworth, statement in the series 'Contemporary English Sculptors', *Architectural Association Journal*, vol.45, no.518, April 1930, p.384.

7. Henry Moore, statement in the series 'Contemporary English Sculptors', *Architectural Association Journal*, vol.45, no.519, May 1930, p.408.

8. John Grierson, 'The New Generation in Sculpture', *Apollo*, vol.12, no.71, November 1930, pp.347–51.

Figure 3. Moore *Girl with Clasped Hands* 1930, Cumberland alabaster, British Council (Henry Moore Foundation).

and, in particular, 'his essay on 'Negro Sculpture', [which] stressed the "three-dimensional realisation" that characterised African art and its "truth to materials" ... Fry opened the way to other books and to the realisation of the British Museum'.[9] It seems striking that, even in retrospect, Moore wished to align himself with earlier artists and their commentators in defiance of the trope of the modern artist's construction as rebelling against the preceding generation.

In the British Museum, Moore encountered works from a diversity of cultures. As he said in 1930,

> *the few sculptors of a hundred years or so of Greece no longer blot our eyes to the sculptural achievements of the rest of mankind: Palaeolithic and Neolithic sculpture, Sumerian, Babylonian and Egyptian, Early Greek, Chinese, Etruscan, Indian, Mayan, Mexican and Peruvian, Romanesque, Byzantine and Gothic, Negro, South Sea Island and North American Indian sculpture.*[10]

Viewing the objects through Fry's writing, he discovered in African figures a 'complete plastic freedom', in Fry's words, which was to say that they were conceived completely in three dimensions, not two, imbuing them with vitality, a term which was central to the perception of the modern in cultural objects.

The belief in the determination of 'plastic form' by the material of the object coalesced with the concept of 'signifcant form' expounded by Fry and Bell. 'Finally', wrote Hepworth, 'it is realised that abstract form, the relationship of masses and planes, is that which gives sculptural life'. Though this enabled the realisation that 'a piece of sculpture can be purely abstract', Hepworth retained figuration as she felt it gave the work 'an added significance of emotional value'.[11] The clasped-handed figures produced by both her and Moore demonstrate a sense of containment that is the result of this negotiation of form and content.

9. Quoted in J.J. Sweeney, 'Henry Moore', statement in *Partisan Review*, vol.14, no.2, March–April 1947. Reprinted in P. James (ed.) *Henry Moore on Sculpture*, London: Macdonald, 1966, p.49.

10. Moore 1930.

11. Hepworth, *op.cit.*

Grierson noticed that this younger generation of artists retained the 'new respect of form' with an added 'affection for material which has added a dash of gaiety'. Skeaping and Hepworth worked in a variety of exotic stones and tropical woods – some of which they encountered through explorations of the Science Museum – and the diversity of materials, and their strong and widely ranging colours, were frequently commented on. Kineton Parkes wrote:

> They are greatly interested in materials, particularly John Skeaping, who is a true glyptic practitioner, even to the extent of tackling gem and bibelot work in lapis lazuli, malachite, anhydrite and bloodstone ... Among the hard and soft stones for larger works Skeaping and his wife have explored the possibilities of Portland, Hoptonwood, Hornton, Ancaster, Gervaux, Terneaux, Roman and soap stones, polyphant, serpentine, alabaster and Irish fossil marble, Sicilian jaune lamantine ... [and] at their exhibition at the Beaux Arts Gallery in 1928, Barbara Hepworth exhibited pieces of Pavonasetta, Carrara, Pavian and Pentelic marble.[12]

The list of preferred woods was equally diverse, but was dominated by tropical hardwoods, such as the Acacia used by Skeaping for *Akua-ba* (1931) and the unidentified Burmese wood from which Hepworth's *Infant* was carved in 1929. As has been noted, one critic concluded from the catalogue of Hepworth and Skeaping's 1930 exhibition that 'it sounds at first like a geological and forestry exhibition'.

The exotic origins of their materials related these works to the artefacts of non-Western cultures with which they were frequently displayed. In the 1928 exhibition R.H. Wilenski 'had the sensation of examining works of sculpture in the British Museum' and for another reviewer the show 'suggested a proposed annexe' to the same museum.[13] The *Daily Express* correspondent believed that 'those who care for sculpture in the British Museum are likely ... to be considerably impressed', and he was not far wrong as George Hill of the Coins Department and Lawrence Binyon of the Oriental Collection became patrons of Hepworth and Skeaping. The reception of the artists' works is reflected in the fact that they were bought by collectors of Oriental art, most notably by George Eumorphopoulos. Similarly, at Sidney Burney's gallery the works of Hepworth and Skeaping were shown alongside African sculpture.

Another, crucial, source for the ideology of truth to materials and the resultant significant forms was a concept of nature. In her 1930 statement Hepworth cited the examples of an egg, a pebble or the swelling of a tree to demonstrate nature's precedents in the production of abstract form. Similarly, in *Unit One* in 1934 Moore advocated the observation of natural form and process as a model for the production of sculpture in different media: the character of shells demonstrated how metal might be used, the growth of trees how to carve wood and, he said, 'pebbles and rocks show Nature's way of working stone'. This was reinforced by Ben Nicholson in the same volume when he compared the production of a relief and the shaping of a stone, establishing a parallel between the artist and nature.

The use of pebbles as a formal source was given a very material reality when Moore, Hepworth and Skeaping took to carving small pieces of ironstone which they first retrieved from the beach at Happisburgh in Norfolk during a holiday in 1930. For Moore, the new material 'showed Nature's treatment of stone, and the principle of the opposition of bumps and hollows',[14] and the enthusiasm with which they took it up was revealed by Hepworth when she reported in 1931 that she and Moore had packed four crates with pebbles for transport to London.[15] Around 1934–5, a similar expediency led the three artists to produce sculptures in Cumberland alabaster, boulders of which were dug out of a Cumbrian field by a farmer who sent them to Skeaping.

There was more than convenience and economy in the use of such found stones. It has been suggested that it might signal a deliberate decision to abandon

12. Kineton Parkes, *The Art of Carved Sculpture, Vol. 1: Western Europe, America and Japan*, London, 1931, pp.128–9.

13. Quoted by Sophie Bowness, 'Modernist stone carving in England and "the big view of sculpture"', *Carving Mountains: Modern Stone Sculpture in England 1907–37*, Cambridge, Kettles Yard exh. cat. 1998, p.37.

14. Letter to Arnold Haskell, quoted in Judith Collins, 'Plastic form and truth to materials', ibid., p.28.

15. Letter to Nicholson, p.m. 29 Sept. 1931, Tate Archive 8717.1.1.52.

exotic stones and woods for indigenous materials as a result of a desire to be associated with ideas of national identity or tradition. One might also identify a self-sufficiency that was in accord with the contemporary development of a particular modernist sensibility or consciouness. It is through such considerations that I wish to suggest a concept of the modern, indexed in the work of these sculptors, which is distinct from, but not in conflict with, the usual idea of an international formalism. To expand, one can associate the practice of direct carving with the elevation of the hand-made in modernist visual culture which, continuing a trajectory that included the Arts and Crafts movement and Bloomsbury's faith in a creative individualism, persisted through the 1920s and early 1930s. I want to show that through the craft revival this aspect reso-

Figure 4. Hepworth *Mother and Child* 1934, Cumberland alabaster, Tate (Hepworth Estate).

nated with ideas of a vernacular culture with which the apparent desire for indi-genous stone was consistent.

When Moore and Hepworth reiterated the basic tenets of truth to materials, they were not only echoing Gill's writing on sculpture but also Herbert Read's on pottery. In 1924, Read claimed that pottery epitomised the relationship between material, the individual creator and a vital object through the immediacy of the relationship between the wet clay, the hands of the potter and the pot's final form.

> *A pot ... is the direct expression of the thought or intuition by which the hand is set in action and guided. The subtle varieties of beautiful form ... cease to be beautiful in proportion as they diverge from the forms which clay may be required to assume without violence to its nature.* [16]

The proximity of Read's rhetoric to contemporary sculptural theory is clear. Similarly, a comparable elevation of the hand-made informed the design of the book *Unit One,* which included photographs of the hands of each artist.

There were strong links between the painters and sculptors of the Moore–Hepworth milieu and contemporary potters. In 1927 and 1928 William Staite Murray, one of the major figures of the British Studio Pottery movement, shared joint exhibitions with Ben Nicholson, who proposed him for membership of the modernist Seven and Five Society.[17] Similarly, Bernard Leach's pots stood, with their Chinese precursors, alongside the sculptures of Hepworth and Skeaping in Eumorphopoulos's collection, and in 1930 the potter held an exhibition at the Beaux Arts Gallery, where the younger artists had shown two years previously.

In any case, the sculptors would certainly have been aware of the potters' attempt to establish a vital contemporary ceramic practice through the synthe-

16. Herbert Read and Bernard Rackham, *English Pottery: Its Development from Early Times to the End of the Eighteenth Century,* London: Ernest Benn, 1924, p.4–5.

17. Malcolm Haslam, *William Staite Murray,* London, 1984.

sis of early Oriental and pre-industrial English techniques and forms. Leach, Staite Murray and others sought to counter what was seen as the deterioration of ceramics through industrialisation by revitalising a vernacular tradition with alien practices and forms of spirituality, and a reassertion of the individualism of the potter. They combined a belief in self-sufficiency, truth to materials, tradition and utility with their search to raise the status of their craft and their pots. To do this, they emphasised the individuality of the maker – considering the potter an artist and equating the pots with sculptures.

The principles upon which the emphasis on individual creativity and the hand-made were based derived in large part from the craft traditions and religions of the Far East. However, they were also conceived in terms of the revival of English slipware, a tradition of 'peasant work' that was thought to have been lost in the Industrial Revolution.[18] Leach and Murray's revival of hand-made ceramics was part of a broader movement that was further strengthened by the publication of Herbert Read and Bernard Rackham's history of pre-nineteenth-century English Pottery. Despite his later position as the principal advocate of an international modern art (and of internationalism more generally), this was one of several books by Read that concentrated on traditional English visual culture. Read presented a primitive, largely rustic English tradition that, implicitly, offered a model for contemporary art. Indeed, his characterisation of the maker of early Staffordshire figures anticipated constructions of Alfred Wallis, who emerged at the same time as a model for Nicholson and Christopher Wood. Comparing these potters to Douanier Rousseau, Read described 'a peasant ... [who] because of [a] simple sense ... often strays unconsciously into a realm of pure forms'. A tradition of hand-made pottery was thus positioned at the centre of the broader revival of early English visual culture, which was marked by such events as the Victoria and Albert Museum's 1930 exhibition of medieval English art. This interest was echoed by Henry Moore when he cited the eleventh-century figure carvings on a Yorkshire church as an early influence.[19]

With *English Pottery* Read and Rackham set out to correct previous histories of English ceramics in which 'the work of the potters who, with less costly stuff, sought to meet the needs of everyday life in the home, was not thought worthy of study' and 'the wares which are of purest English blood' were ignored for the foreign-inspired products of manufacturers such as

18. For the contemporary use of the phrase see Edmund de Waal, *Bernard Leach*, London: Tate, 1997, p.32.

19. Henry Moore, 'Primitive Art', *Listener*, vol.25, no.641, 24 Aug. 1941, pp.598–9.

Figure 5. Leach Pottery coffee set, 1930s (Leach Estate).

Wedgwood. They identified in the pots 'a national character', and this theme was adopted after the Second World War by George Wingfield Digby, who believed the common forms shared by medieval and modern English pottery were determined by their indigenous materials:

> the English potter has the sense of working with his own natural materials ... He is producing something directly from his own native soil, vegetation and rocks. Like the English mediaeval potter ... his is what may rightly be termed ... an essentially indigenous art.[20]

The parallel with the sculptors' use of locally retrieved stone is clear.

Thus, one might see the sculpture of the 1920s and early 1930s within a broader belief in the redemptive powers of the hand-made, itself the key to the production of a vital art. In this light, the retention of the claw marks in Hepworth's *Figure of a Woman* (1929–30) becomes more than a schematic depiction of hair as it makes evident the artist's working process. I would like to expand this investigation to suggest a way in which this theorisation of the objects might reveal how they operated within the modern environment. This aspect might allow us to carry what has gone before forward into the later part of the 1930s.

A correlation was established by Leach between the traditional hand-made methods and functionalism of pre-industrial pottery and a traditional rural domesticity, and he explicitly created a link between an English identity and this domestic sphere. In retrospect, he recalled the Japanese response to his work in the 1930s: '"We admire your stoneware – influenced by the East"', they told him, '"but we love your English slipware – *born not made*". That sank home', he said, 'and ... determined us to counterbalance the exhibition of expensive personal pottery by a basic production of what we called domestic ware'.[21] It was this domestic, or standard, ware which J.P. Hodin would later describe as 'warm in character ... and homely in colour ... suitable for honey, treacle, cream – that is to say for simple, country life, the extreme opposite to life in the metropolis'.[22] Leach had recognised this in his summary of the work of the 1920s which, he wrote, 'expressed the English national temperament of one or two hundred years ago ... Its earthy and homely nature belongs to the kitchen, the cottage, and the country ... it only harmonises with the whitewash, oak, iron, leather, and pewter of "Old England"'.[23]

I want to argue that the world implicit in Read and Rackham's account of English pottery, and with which Leach associated his own production, was seen to provide a model for modern life. It was based upon a form of rural domesticity which Ben and Winifred Nicholson actively sought to replicate in the 1920s. At Bankshead, their home in Cumberland, they chose a simple existence, mixing in their domestic environment traditional furnishings with contemporary works of art. Photographs reveal how the work of artists such as Piet Mondrian and Alfred Wallis punctuated the world of oak settles and Windsor chairs, while a rug made to Ben Nicholson's design covered the flagstones in front of the kitchen range. It was, as Harrison has said, a 'modernist fantasy' and closely echoed the deliberately nostalgic illustrations of books such as Gertrude Jekyll's *Old English Household Life* of 1926.[24]

Echoing Read's writing on English slipware, Jekyll lamented the loss of a rural craft tradition: 'Lost is the spirit that once pervaded the village homes and brought vitality, form and purpose to labours and workmanship set in country places. Personal expression, interpreted through the cunning of human hands ... now ceases to have the place it once held'. It was just this demise of an English domestic handicraft tradition that motivated potters like Leach and Murray, and echoes of it might be discerned in the ideology of direct carving. That Gill was so closely associated with other participants in this craft revival, such as the Ditchling-based weaver Ethel Mairet, further supports the suggestion.

20. George Wingfield Digby, *The Work of the Modern Potter in England*, London: John Murray, 1952, p.13.

21. Bernard Leach, *Beyond East and West*, London: Faber & Faber, 1978/1985, p.146.

22. J.P. Hodin, *Bernard Leach: A Potter's Work*, Bath, 1967, p.25.

23. Bernard Leach, *A Potter's Outlook*, Handworkers Pamphlet No.3, New Handworkers' Gallery, London, 1928, p.33.

24. Charles Harrison, 'Ben Nicholson and the Decline of Cubism', lecture at the Tate Gallery, 1993.

A glimpse of the domestic environment at Bankshead is of more than anecdotal interest. I believe that we should not see the art of the Seven and Five circle in terms of a pictorial or sculptural modernism in isolation, but as part of a wider desire to modernise everyday life. The Nicholsons' response to modernity was the development of a new consciousness which encompassed a new life-style and new spirituality as much as new cultural forms. Like Paul and Margaret Nash, they both believed in Christian Science, a new faith which established a unity between God and individual subjectivity. In line with this, they pursued a simple life of abstract belief, vegetarianism and an optimistic view of modernity. Winifred Nicholson's later recollection of the period encapsulates their attitude to life: 'Boundaries and barriers were broken down – and the vista ahead was light-hearted. We lived in white houses with large windows, we ate simple foods – the fruits of the earth. We wore sandals and ran barefoot along the boulevards. We talked in the cafés of the new vision'. Thus modern ideas and culture – the fascination with light that informed the International Style of architecture, for instance – were combined with the simplicity and spiritual integrity of a past rural existence. During the 1930s Hepworth also adopted much of the rhetoric of Christian Science. This is reflected in her statement in *Unit One*, dominated by the terms 'lovely' and 'loveliness', in which she wrote: 'The predisposition to carve is not enough, there must be a positive living and moving towards an ideal.'

The fascination with rusticity was not simply the pursuit of individual integration through a retreat to an idealised rural past, but, I would suggest, the proposition of a modernist view based upon the domestic rather than the public realm. Since Baudelaire's description of the flâneur, modern art and architecture may generally have suppressed the domestic sphere, but I propose that here it was central. In the later 1920s, the domestic scene became a staple theme for such modern British painters as David Jones, Ivon Hitchens, Christopher Wood and the Nicholsons, and even the landscape was generally framed within a window and viewed through a still-life arrangement.

I have argued elsewhere that one can see the foregrounding of the hand-made and, by association, of the domestic sphere carried through into the non-figurative works of Ben Nicholson, even into the white reliefs that he produced from 1934. These were carved from wood, scraped down and painted with household paint in a process which he compared to the scrubbing of a kitchen table. The artist sought to highlight the fact that the finish of many of them was uneven, the apparently flat white surfaces actually modulated by the grain of the wood and the chisel marks that stand as testimony to the carving of the panel. Herbert Read used this quality to refute Kenneth Clark's criticism of modern art's 'fatal defect of purity', emphasising the fact that the reliefs were 'carved with hammer and chisel out of woods like walnut and mahogany', and explaining that they were subjective expressions of nature determined by 'the senses of the artist reacting to a plastic material' just as the forms of natural organisms are moulded by 'sun and soil'. Despite the abandonment of figuration for purer forms, one can see Hepworth's persistent carving (which is in contrast to Moore's departure into lead casting during the 1930s) as indicative of her desire to retain the same qualities in her sculpture. From 1935 (not 1934 as the artist claimed), her work was dominated by simple abstract forms, often arrayed across a surface, the harmonious disposition providing a spatial parallel to Nicholson's compositions. However, the forms are always a little off true and the demonstrable traces of their carving retain a human dimension.

Works such as Nicholson's reliefs and Hepworth's *Conoid Sphere and Hollow* were exhibited and photographed in a number of the presentations of the modern domestic environment, such as Duncan Miller's 'Modern Pictures for Modern Homes' exhibition of 1936 and Leslie and Sadie Martin's *The Flat Book*

Figure 6. Barbara Hepworth *Conoid, Sphere and Hollow,* 1937, marble, Government Art Collections (Hepworth Estate) 1937.

(1939). One might see the proclaimed hand-madeness of the art as a means of bringing into the modern home the suggestion of the past, rural domestic environment. Read employed the no-nonsense functionalism of pre-industrial English domestic items as reassuring and exemplary precedents for modern design in his book *Art and Industry* (1934). Sixteenth-and seventeenth-century cutlery, pottery and glass were juxtaposed with modern continental equivalents and a Windsor chair was set up as the epitome of simple elegance. Thus the furniture of Jekyll's nostalgic rural life was employed to humanise and validate modernist design. It is my conjecture that the works of such artists as Nicholson and Hepworth, through their essential hand-made quality, like the pots of Leach and Staite Murray or the fabrics of Mairet, could have served a similar purpose.

None of this is to challenge those qualities which have generally been seen to define sculpture of the period as modern. Nor is it to undermine the internationalism claimed for modernism in this period. Rather, my hope has been to try to dislodge the monolithic understanding of modernism and to suggest ways in which what is perceived as traditional culture, as part of a new consciousness in defiance of industrial materialism, also played a key role in the formulation of a sculptural practice that addressed the experience of modernity.

3 NEW EYES FOR OLD: ARCHITECTURAL PHOTOGRAPHY

ROBERT ELWALL

NEW EYES FOR OLD: ARCHITECTURAL PHOTOGRAPHY[1]

ROBERT ELWALL

In a discerning article written for the *Architectural Review* in 1934 and significantly entitled 'New Eyes for Old', the critic Philip Morton Shand paid tribute to the unique relationship between modern architecture and the New Photography, writing,

> Did modern photography beget modern architecture or the converse?... since their logical development was simultaneous, and their interaction considerable, it hardly matters which. What does matter is that it was the same sort of mind and power of vision which has produced both; and that both are based on abstract form ... In the early 1920's architectural photography was as unimaginatively true to 'life' and conventional perspective as any other sort of photography. Men with the cultural equipment of beach photographers walked round buildings at a respectful distance like policemen on their beat flashing lanterns on the impeccably obvious. But the new sort of architects had their buildings taken by the new sort of photographers. A revolution in the technique of architectural photography resulted, which has revolutionized architectural criticism.[2]

Yet only 11 years earlier the architect and photographer T.H.B. Scott had lamented, 'Architectural photography is at a very low ebb'... We yearn for good photographic appreciation of modern architectural expression.[3] How did this transformation come about, what were its chief characteristics and who were its main protagonists?

By the time Scott was writing two divergent streams of architectural photography had emerged. One, which might be termed pictorial, had its origins in the images made by amateur photographers and fledgling professionals such as Francis Bedford in the 1850s whose choice of subject matter – predominantly the ruined architecture of the past – was dictated by picturesque conventions, and whose approach was heavily influenced by the English topographical watercolour tradition. The aim was less to analyse architectural form, more to use buildings as starting points for musings on the ravages of time or the inevitability of transience and thereby enhance photography's claim to be art. This meant above all ignoring what one critic termed 'spick and span modern buildings'.[4] This tradition of architectural photography was revived around the turn of the century by the great Linked Ring photographer, Frederick Evans, some of whose work appeared in *Country Life*, the magazine which more than any other continued to use this softly lit, atmospheric photographic style. In photography generally pictorialism was in the ascendancy until the First World War.

The other, more mainstream tradition of architectural photography was that of professionals such as Bedford Lemere & Co. whose work was commissioned by clients, builders, decorators and architects. The aim of these photographers was not to essay expressive or dramatic compositions but rather to provide cogent documentary records. Accordingly they preferred to work under neutral skies, often early in the morning, when vital details would not be obscured by shadow and to utilise small lens apertures to ensure the sharp

Figure 1. Dell & Wainwright. Sun-catch, House A, Whipsnade (1936). Architects: Lubetkin & Tecton (RIBA Library Photographs Collection).

1. This article is a revised version of the paper given at the *Modern Britain 1929–1939* conference held at the Courtauld Institute, London, 5 March, 1999 and draws on material to be found in my *Photography Takes Command: the Camera and British Architecture 1890–1939*, London, RIBA Heinz Gallery, 1994, which investigates the issues raised here in greater detail. Those wishing to explore the British scene in an international context are directed to my *Building with Light: the International History of Architectural Photography*, London, Merrell, 2004.

2. *Architectural Review*, vol.75, Jan. 1934, p.12.

3. T. H. B. Scott, 'Architecture in Relation to Pictorial Photography', *Building News*, vol.125, 21 Dec. 1923, pp.688–689.

4. *Journal of the Photographic Society*, vol.3, 21 May 1857, p.276.

definition and legibility over the entire image area their clients demanded. Considered commercial and mechanical the resultant photographs were banished to the backwater technical sections of photographic exhibitions.

Throughout the 19th century the influence of the photograph on architectural design and criticism, though great, was limited by the continued vitality of architectural rendering in other media, such as Orlando Jewitt's evocative woodcuts in *The Builder* or the photolithographic reproduction of designs by architects such as Richard Norman Shaw, who honed his drawing technique specifically to such reproduction. Most of all, however, the photograph's influence was limited by its incompatibility with the printing press. The introduction of half-tone printing in the 1890s, which allowed photographs to be

Figure 2. Bedford Lemere & Co., Palace Theatre, London (1891). Architect: T. E. Collcutt (RIBA Library Photographs Collection).

Figure 3. Eric Mendelsohn, Shelton Hotel, New York. Photogravure from *Amerika* (1926) (RIBA Library Books & Periodicals Collection).

reproduced alongside type for the first time, therefore revolutionised architectural photography. Magazines such as the *Architectural Review* (1896) and *Country Life* (1897), which were established to exploit the new technology, were henceforth to be the prime movers in the development of the genre, lending enhanced status to photographic illustrations, patronising the leading photographers, and enabling their imagery to be seen by a much wider audience albeit in reproduction and subject to the dictates of art editors. Although photographers increasingly geared print production to magazines' needs, these developments were not, however, accompanied by any major changes in the way buildings were photographed.

The catalyst for change was the emergence after the First World War of a new vision in Europe, particularly in Germany, and the United States which by paying increased attention to the man-made rather than the natural world helped to revitalise architectural photography. The new post-war order was to be created by industry, revealed in a machine-inspired architecture and evangelised by the photographer. Anathema to pictorialist photographers, images of contemporary architecture and engineering such as the spare, analytical studies of New Objectivity photographers like Werner Mantz or those by Charles Sheeler of the Ford Plant at River Rouge, Detroit, now moved centre stage and were presented as icons of this brave new world. At the same time the introduction of more versatile cameras, especially the Leica in 1924, encouraged experimentation with different points of view and a fresh appraisal of architectural form. Close-ups, worm's- and bird's-eye views characterised the so-called New Photography, revealing novel and more dynamic possibilities for photographing buildings beyond the standard one-or two-point perspective. A good example is provided by the photographs the architect Erich Mendelsohn took for his book *Amerika* (1926), of which El Lissitzky wrote, 'Leafing through the pages for the first time grips us like a dramatic film. Completely strange pictures unwind before our eyes. You have to hold the book over your head and twist it around to understand some of the photographs. The architect shows us America, not from the distance, but from the inside; he leads us through the canyons of its streets'.[5] László Moholy-Nagy similarly used distorted perspective views to provide 'new experiences of space ... With their help, and that of the new school of architects', he declared, 'we have an enlargement and sublimation of our appreciation of space, the comprehension of a new spatial culture'.[6] Three further factors encouraged this exploration of new viewpoints. First, there was the practical necessity of simply pointing the camera skywards to record ever taller buildings. Second, there was the development of aviation and aerial reconnaissance which saw the emergence of the first firms specialising in aerial photography including British Aerofilms Ltd (1919) and which prompted Le Corbusier to claim in his 1935 book *Aircraft*, 'By means of the airplane, we now have proof, recorded on the photographic plate, of the rightness of our desire to alter methods of architecture and town-planning'.[7] Third, there was the influence of the cinema and in particular a number of films such as Walter Ruttmann's *Berlin, the Symphony of a Great City* (1927), which explored urban space in novel ways.

In addition to unconventional viewpoints, the New Photography also stressed radical cropping and vigorous tonal contrasts. The cinema's influence could again be felt in the New Photography's experimentation with photomontage and the way in which photographers increasingly juxtaposed elements within the frame to advance arguments either by contrast or comparison, as well as in their increased readiness to think in terms of narrative sequences of images rather than single shots. As *Modern Photography* reported in 1932,

> *The possibilities of views looking down, of views looking up, of extreme perspectives, of space dramatically conceived, the turning of the tables in scale by which a small object, suitably lighted, becomes dignified and impressive, and a large one, rendered small, takes on a new relation to its surroundings, all these things have been formed into a technical repertoire unknown to the photographer in the days before the war.* [8]

These new trends only slowly became evident in Britain and then in a diluted form which paralleled the similar reception architectural modernism was accorded by British architects. There are, for example, only fleeting glimpses of the New Photography in the work of F.R. Yerbury, the most influential British architectural photographer of the 1920s. His images published in the *Architect & Building News* to accompany a series of more than 150 articles by Howard Robertson played a crucial role in acquainting many British architects with the exciting architectural developments that were taking place abroad, but it was Mark Oliver Dell and H.L. Wainwright, official photographers to the *Architectural Review* from 1930 to 1946, who were primarily responsible for the marriage of modern architecture to an appropriately modern style of photography. Their debut in the *Architectural Review* was made in 1929 with coverage of Raymond McGrath's Finella at Cambridge. These Finella photographs are markedly different from the usual run-of-the-mill journal illustrations of the period and their expressive camera angles and dramatic use of light and shadow were to become hallmarks of the duo's work. Even though professional photographers continued to use stand cameras – and these images were, in fact, taken on a half-plate Sanderson – they do nevertheless show the liberating effect hand-held cameras such as the Leica, which Dell and Wainwright used extensively in news photography for the BBC, had on architectural

5. Quoted in Beaumont Newhall, *The History of Photography from 1839 to the Present*, London, Secker & Warburg, 1982, p.11.

6. László Moholy-Nagy, 'A New Instrument of Vision', *Telehor*, vol.1, Feb. 1936, p.36.

7. Le Corbusier, *Aircraft*, London, The Studio, 1935, p.11.

8. Studio Annual, *Modern Photography*, ed. C. G. Holme, London, The Studio, 1932, p.11.

photography. As McGrath, who claimed to have discovered the photographers, admiringly wrote, 'All day they pursued shadows over the floors and furniture, all night they made moons rise and created other elusive phenomena with their arc lamps. They competed in style with my lighting effects. It was better than Pyramus and Thisbe.'[9] Although their partnership lasted for only 16 years Dell and Wainwright transformed the face of British architectural photography, establishing the norm that most other photographers would follow until the 1960s, and, by popularising modern architecture, underlined the camera's power and influence.

Very little is known about Wainwright but Dell's background surprisingly lay in the pictorial photographic tradition. He had been secretary to the pho-

Figure 4. Francis Rowland Yerbury. Sprinkenhof, Hamburg (1929). Architects: Fritz Höger with Hans and Oskar Gerson (RIBA Library Photographs Collection).

Figure 5. Dell & Wainwright. Highpoint I, Highgate, London (1935). Architects: Lubetkin & Tecton (RIBA Library Photographs Collection).

Figure 6. Dell & Wainwright. Finella, Cambridge (1929). Architect: Raymond McGrath (Architectural Press Archive / RIBA Library Photographs Collection).

9. *Finella Collection*, Caius College Archives, Cambridge. Quoted in Alan Powers, 'Simple Intime – the Work of Raymond McGrath', *Thirties Society Journal*, no.3, 1982, p.5.

10. *Photographic Journal*, vol.100, Jan. 1960, p.36.

tographic society of the Hampshire House Trust, a social club organised on temperance lines for the poor of Fulham. Here he encountered Herbert Felton, who was also to become one of the leading architectural photographers of the 1930s, and the internationally renowned photographer Alvin Langdon Coburn. In 1921 he became a founder member of the Royal Photographic Society's Pictorial Group, which was implacably opposed to the New Photography, and submitted photographs described by Felton as 'dreamy sunsets, limpid sunrises, flour mills disguised as ancient castles'[10] which were very much in the style of Alexander Keighley, one of Britain's leading pictorial photographers whom Dell greatly admired. During the 1920s, however, a change came over Dell's landscape work which became progressively less impressionistic and showed him taking a greater interest in architectonic form. In 1923 he set up in business with Wainwright and in 1926 they were appointed photographers to the BBC, a post which proved a testing bed for their work for the *Architectural Review*.

This work bears all the characteristic hallmarks of the New Photography and helped to establish the *Architectural Review* as the most innovative architectural magazine of the period. Their image of the *Daily Express* building,

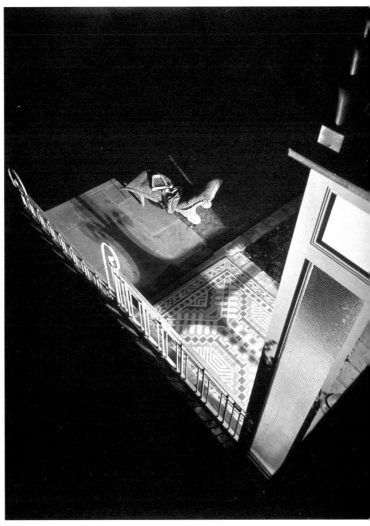

Fleet Street (1931), was shot obliquely from below not only to emphasise the black vitrolite and glass cladding but also to allow the inclusion of the steeple of Wren's St Bride's, thus artfully suggesting that here was a worthy modernist successor to Wren's church. A similar stratagem of juxtaposition – and one that was to become a cliché of modernist photography – can also be seen in their view of Ramsgate Municipal Airport (1937), where the fuselage of the plane in the foreground counterpoises the terminal building beyond to emphasise the machine aesthetic of the new architecture.

Figure 7. Dell & Wainwright, Ramsgate Municipal Airport (1937). Architect: David Pleydell-Bouverie (RIBA Library Photographs Collection).

Figure 8. Dell & Wainwright. *Daily Express* Building, London (1931). Architect: Sir Owen Williams (Architectural Press Archive / RIBA Library Photographs Collection).

It was in their photography of interiors that Dell and Wainwright's imagery was at its most expressive. This was achieved principally through the bold use of theatrical lighting and strong cast shadow that could lend an almost surrealistic feel to their work. They were also quick to exploit the dramatic new possibilities afforded by reflective materials such as mirror glass and chromium which were favoured by modernist architects, while their extended coverage of the RIBA's new headquarters (1934) was deliberately cinematic in its presentation, with an adroitly conceived sequence of close-ups and reverse-angle shots being employed to explore the building's spatial relationships. As Moholy-Nagy suggested, the intimation of space was now a priority for photographers rather than the portrayal of mass and ornament that had dominated the output of their 19th century forbears.

During the 1930s, as the debate for and against modern architecture intensified, the *Architectural Review* became increasingly committed to the modernist cause. Dell and Wainwright's photographs were central to its efforts to sell modernism to a sceptical public and profession and it is they more than

Figure 9. Dell & Wainwright, House on the Aldwick Bay Estate, Bognor Regis (1935). Architect: Stuart Cameron Kirby (Architectural Press Archive / RIBA Library Photographs Collection).

Figure 10. Dell & Wainwright, Flats, Cranley Court, Cranley Gardens, London (1933). Architect: Stuart Cameron Kirby (Architectural Press Archive / RIBA Library Photographs Collection).

Figure 11. Dell & Wainwright, Bathroom for Tilly Losch, 35 Wimpole Street, London (1933). Designer: Paul Nash (Architectural Press Archive / RIBA Library Photographs Collection).

Figure 12. Dell & Wainwright, Royal Institute of British Architects, London (1934). Architect: George Grey Wornum (Architectural Press Archive / RIBA Library Photographs Collection).

Figure 13. Dell & Wainwright. Gull Rock, Carlyon Bay (1936). Architect: Marshall Sisson (RIBA Library Photographs Collection).

anyone else who are responsible for our enduring image of 1930s architecture of flat-roofed, horizontal-windowed, box-shaped houses, which, often accentuated by the photographers' use of coloured filters, glisten white and immaculate under louring skies. The view of Marshall Sisson's Gull Rock, Carlyon Bay (1936), is a typical example of how a modest house portrayed in this way could assume a heroic dimension. Similarly their view of the sun-catch at House A, Whipsnade, by Lubetkin and Tecton (1936), which prefigures Julius Shulman's celebrated documentation of California's post-war Case Study houses, demonstrates that the product to be sold was not simply architecture but lifestyle. Defying the picturesque conventions which had informed the image-making of early architectural photographers and their pictorialist successors, these houses were also usually photographed detached from their landscape context and while still new, before any planting had taken effect, thus reinforcing the landscape gardener Geoffrey Jellicoe's observation that 'the modern architect will see the house as a white bird, descended from the sky and perched upon the green fields'.[11] These were utopian images that by concentrating on pure form with relief and modelling provided by strong cast shadow sought to proclaim the triumph of man and machine over nature. With the passage of time, however, the gap became ever wider between the fixed image of refulgent, virginal white forms bathed in sunlight that became so familiar to readers of the *Architectural Review* and the sadly deteriorating reality of staining of materials, leaking roofs and other structural faults to which Modern Movement houses frequently fell prey. Nevertheless, as the *Architects' Journal* maintained, these images 'played a large part in popularizing modern architecture; by bringing out its glamour and charm they made it easier for those who judge solely by appearances to accept it while its practical principles were being established'.[12]

The New Photography was perhaps to be seen at its most starkly graphic in the work of John Havinden, who though not an architectural photographer *per se* contributed some of the *Architectural Review*'s most mesmerising images. Havinden's career illustrates how one of the main driving forces behind the New Photography was the advertising industry. His brother, Ashley, was not only a noted graphic artist and textile designer but also a director of Crawfords

11. Geoffrey Jellicoe. *Garden Decoration and Ornament for Smaller Houses,* London, Country Life Ltd, 1936, p.5.

12. *Architects' Journal,* vol.103, 13 June 1946, p.445.

Advertising Agency and this connection, together with his friendship with leading avant-garde designers and architects such as Edward McKnight Kauffer and Wells Coates, secured a string of commissions for John Havinden's company Gretton Studios. His client list, which included HMV and GEC, reads like a roll-call of the progressive firms of the day and his wonderful photograph of Wells Coates' Lawn Road flats, Hampstead (1934), was taken as a product shot to advertise Crittall's metal windows. Best of all were his images of Lubetkin and Tecton's zoo buildings which expressively conveyed the sculptural plasticity of the concrete used, especially the photograph of the Penguin Pool, London Zoo (1934). A testament to this photograph's potency was its use by Hollywood mogul David O. Selznick to recreate the pool for his film comedy *The Young in Heart* in 1938.

Figure 14. Dell & Wainwright. Shangri-la, Lee-on-Solent (1937). Architect: F. R. S. Yorke (RIBA Library Photographs Collection).

Figure 15. John Havinden. Penguin Pool, London Zoo (1934). Architects: Lubetkin & Tecton (RIBA Library Photographs Collection).

The seductive appeal of these photographs was greatly enhanced by the inventive ways in which they were laid out on the *Architectural Review*'s pages. The look of the magazine was strongly influenced by German illustrated magazines of the 1920s, such as the *Münchner Illustrierte Presse*, which pioneered photojournalism, and the French periodical *Arts et Métiers*, first published in 1927. The *Architectural Review*'s owner and editor, Hubert de Cronin Hastings, also played a major role with his maxims that each page should contain a surprise and that general views should be reproduced small and details large. The conservative 'window' reproduction of photographs, still the standard in other magazines of the period, was jettisoned for a more radical approach that resulted in images being bled to the edge of the page or even beyond in fold-out sheets. There were also experiments with four-colour printing and photographs were frequently overlaid with explanatory drawings. The photograph thus became a fully integrated element of the magazine rather than a mere illustrative appendage. This fertile experimentation can be seen at its most daring in the July 1936 special issue, 'Leisure at the Seaside', which the high priest of the New Photography, Moholy-Nagy, who had recently sought refuge in England, was commissioned to design and illustrate.

Complementing the *Architectural Review*'s formal set-piece photography were the lively, amateur snapshots taken with small format cameras by editorial staff and freelance contributors such as the architects Bryan and Norman Westwood, and the artists Paul Nash and John Piper, which served to enlarge the range of subject matter deemed suitable for photographic scrutiny. These images were used in polemical fashion to highlight key concerns of the magazine such as the despoliation of the countryside by insensitive development or the unfettered suburban sprawl condemned in the 1938 'Towns in Transition' series. They also allowed a readier scrutiny of previously neglected aspects of architectural heritage than was possible with the use of a professional stand camera, which implied a high level of planning and premeditation. In articles such as 'The Nautical Style'[13] and 'Black and White; an Introductory Study of a National Design Idiom',[14] for example, Piper's photographs highlighted the simple propriety of vernacular structures such as lighthouses and nonconformist chapels which he and the editor, Jim Richards, had explored together. These unaffected snapshots became an important component of architectural journalism, especially after the war, in the work, for example, of Ian Nairn. Similarly their subject matter prefigured Eric de Maré's concern to document Britain's 'functional tradition' which in turn influenced the work of architects such as James Stirling.

In other magazines the influence of the New Photography may have been less pronounced but a steady growth in the number of architectural titles during the period saw competition intensify and a concomitant raising of the standards of photographic reproduction. In addition, in an era when there was considerable public interest in architecture, the readily intelligible photograph was seen as a more potent means of presenting architecture to a lay audience than the more recondite architectural drawing. Finally, in a prescient comment that presaged the ever-more unseemly haste with which journals today strive to be the first to cover new buildings, often to the detriment of considered, interpretative photography, the architect Goodhart-Rendel astutely observed that the photograph was, 'not only illustration but news'.[15] The upshot was that the style of photography pioneered by Dell and Wainwright influenced even their more conventional *confrères* such as Sydney Newbery and Leo Herbert Felton.

13. *Architectural Review*, vol.83, Jan. 1938.

14. *Architectural Review*, vol 82, 1937 Nov

15. *Architect & Building News*, vol.150, 9 Apr 1937, p.33.

Figure 16. Page spread from *Architectural Review*, March 1939, showing house in Newton Road, London, with photographs by Alfred Cracknell. Architect: Denys Lasdun (RIBA Library Books & Periodicals Collection).

Figure 17. John Piper. Lighthouse, Dungeness from *Architectural Review*, January 1938 (RIBA Library Books & Periodicals Collection).

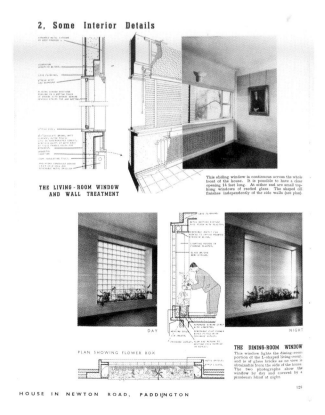

Official photographer to the *Architects' Journal* from 1920 to 1935, Newbery hailed from a family of lithographers and had served in the Royal Flying Corps in the First World War and then as an aerial photographer in the White Russian campaign of 1919. By 1959, when an exhibition of his photographs was held at the RIBA, he reckoned to have taken over 200,000 architectural views. Described by Sir John Summerson as 'rather severe ... the model of a professional man',[16] Newbery was a superb technician as, for example, his photograph of Raymond McGrath's Fischer's Restaurant of 1933 illustrates. His use of 8 × 6 or 10 × 12 inch glass plates ensured that his photographs were characterised by their tremendous definition and stylistically, while the majority were in the

Figure 18. Sydney Newbery. Fischer's Restaurant, London (1933). Architect: Raymond McGrath (RIBA Library Photographs Collection).

Figure 19. Leo Herbert Felton. High & Over, Amersham (1930). Architects: Connell & Ward (Architectural Press Archive / RIBA Library Photographs Collection).

documentary manner of Bedford Lemere, the influence of the New Photography became increasingly apparent. A contemporary described his work as 'absolutely dead reliable. Photos as glossy as you needed and glass hard.'[17]

The *Architects' Journal*'s weekly rival, the *Architect & Building News*, regularly commissioned one of the finest photographers of the decade in Herbert Felton, whose career followed a path similar to that of Dell's. While throughout the 1930s he regularly photographed modernist buildings, such as Connell and Ward's High and Over, Amersham (1930), for various leading architectural magazines, he was at the same time one of the most active members of the Royal Photographic Society Pictorial Group, indulging his passion for photographing churches and the Norfolk landscape. Sir John Summerson, who was assistant editor of the *Architect & Building News*, recalled that Felton had 'an incorrigible preference for picturesque views over disciplined recording'[18] – hardly surprising as Felton was a great friend and admirer of Frederick Evans, whose work he once fondly described as 'not so much photographs of actual places, but rather as pictures imbued with the spirit and atmosphere peculiar to each building'.[19] Looking at Felton's architectural photographs of the 1930s it is hard to detect the picturesque tendency that worried Summerson. Rather, Felton emerges as a skilled interpreter of modernism even if like, Dell, he was later to return to the pictorialist subjects he found more congenial.

16. Letter from Sir John Summerson to the author, Jan. 1988.

17. Quoted in manuscript history of the Architectural Press. I am grateful to Peter Davey for allowing me to consult this.

18. Letter from Sir John Summerson to the author, Jan. 1988.

19. Herbert Felton, 'Photographer's Foreword', in John Harvey, *The English Cathedrals*, London, Batsford, 1950, p.vii.

Some of the images most redolent of the period were taken by the Liverpool-born photographer John Maltby, whose lucrative commission from the Odeon cinema chain to take four photographs of each cinema it built for a fixed fee of £3 was instrumental in establishing his reputation as an architectural and industrial photographer of the first rank. As can be seen by his arresting shot of a floodlit Battersea A power station Maltby was especially adept at night photography, which really came of age in the 1930s and greatly extending the dramatic options available to the photographer.

The number of highly proficient architectural photographers working during the 1930s – to those already mentioned could be added Edward Stewart

Figure 20. John Maltby. Battersea Power Station, London (1935). Designers: Sir Giles Gilbert Scott and James Theodore Halliday (RIBA Library Photographs Collection).

Bale, Humphrey and Vera Joel, Millar and Harris – is indicative of the genre's new-found vitality and importance. This growing importance was quickly seized upon by architects who recognised that journals and photographic re-productions could be key means of promoting their work. Architects thus be-came keener not only to ensure their buildings were photographed by empathetic photographers but also to have a greater say in how they were pho-tographed. Photography had simply become too important to be left to the photographer alone. Underlying this increased desire for control was a new recognition that photography was not merely a mechanical but a creative act involving choices and different possible outcomes – a recognition prompted in part by the more expressive New Photography and the growing use of bylines which together highlighted the often divergent approaches of individual pho-tographers. It was the architect's task, therefore, to ensure the photographer portrayed his building in the best possible light. Thus the period witnessed the development of close collaborations between architects and their favoured photographers – in France, for example, between Le Corbusier and Marius Gravot; in Germany between Wilhelm Riphahn and Werner Mantz; in Holland between J.J.P. Oud and Evert van Ojen; in America between Richard Neutra and Julius Shulman; and in Britain between Berthold Lubetkin and Maltby, a relationship buttressed by their shared socialist beliefs.

Figure 21. Dell & Wainwright. Joldwynds, Holmbury St Mary (1933). Architect: Oliver Hill (RIBA Library Photographs Collection).

The British architect who during the inter-war years perhaps best exempli-fied this new trend was the chameleon-like Oliver Hill, whose buildings, while wide-ranging stylistically, were consistently photogenic, from the expression-ist fantasy of Maryland, Hurtwood (1930), to the sleek modernity of the Mid-land Hotel, Morecambe (1933). Hill may have been inspired by the example of Sir Edwin Lutyens whom he greatly admired and whose work had been ar-dently championed by *Country Life*. The *Country Life* connection also proved invaluable to Hill who recalled,

> *The first house I built attracted the discerning eye of Edward Hudson,*
> *the founder of the paper, and although he enquired about its architect*
> *we did not meet till much later. I knew Sleigh, however, his chief photo-*
> *grapher, who took some splendid pictures for me that came to the notice*
> *of Lawrence Weaver, and after the war I was included in his team to*
> *work on the Wembley exhibition.*[20]

Most importantly the magazine voted Joldwynds, his modernist house at Holmbury St Mary for the barrister Wilfred Greene, its House of the Year for 1933 and published a spectacular series of photographs, orchestrated by Hill. These included a shot of the entrance flanked by statues of two does which crop up again in views of other houses by Hill. Unfortunately Hill's client quickly became exasperated with the structural problems that continued to beset the house, writing acidly to his architect, 'Your job does not come to an end as you seem to think when you have got something that looks nice in a photograph.'[21] Greene's wife was equally outraged by the furniture Hill had designed, 'It would all photograph nicely, including the bookcases when filled, as at your suggestion, with books that no one could read, but which had good bindings. Unfortunately Joldwynds was meant for a house to live in, not a lovely film set.'[22] The story of Joldwynds, which ended with the frustrated Greenes commissioning Tecton to build a new house in its grounds, graphi-cally demonstrates the widening gap between photographic illusion and real-ity that impelled Hugh Casson, when reviewing F.R.S. Yorke's *The Modern House in England* in 1938, to complain, 'Architecture has become the handmaid of photography ... A lot of those houses were images of houses.'[23]

In 1935 the *Architectural Review* referred to 'the ever-increasing debt which architecture owes to the camera',[24] a state of affairs that prompted heightened debate about the nature of architectural photography. What was undeniable however was that the camera was becoming the ubiquitous interpreter and mediator of architectural works. In a sign of the changing times 1930 saw the launch of a new magazine, *Architecture Illustrated*, a monthly notable for be-ing filled almost entirely with photographs, with only the occasional plan and minimal text apart from the captions to the pictures. Exhibitions too were in-creasingly dominated by photographs and even the conservative Royal Acad-emy had been forced to admit them. The pages of *Academy Architecture*, which reproduced the exhibits on show at the RA and which had once been filled solely with drawings, included a higher proportion of photographs each year throughout the 1920s before ceasing publication entirely in 1931. Here was confirmation that the role of the RA in advancing architects' careers was being seriously challenged. With their preference for using models and axonometric drawings which better illustrated the geometrically abstract forms of their de-signs than the more picturesque perspective, Modern Movement architects were excluded from the RA by hidebound hanging committees and conse-quently turned to the journals and photography to proselytise their work. Whereas in the 19th century photographs of 'almost every style under the sun'[25] had fuelled eclecticism, now the camera's imagery was heavily instru-mental in promoting a particular architectural movement. It was, in the words of John Brandon-Jones, 'a propaganda exercise, unparalleled since Burlington brought in the Palladian style',[26] and Shand declared 'without modern photog-

20. Oliver Hill, 'An Architect's Debt to *Country Life*', *Country Life*, vol.141, 12 Jan. 1967, p.70.

21. Letter from Wilfred Greene to Oliver Hill, 26 Nov. 1934 [HiO/16/1], *Oliver Hill Papers*, Archives Collection, British Architectural Library, RIBA

22. Letter from Nancy Greene to Oliver Hill, 21 June 1934 [HiO/16/1], *Oliver Hill Papers*, Archives Collection, British Architectural Library, RIBA

23. *Architectural Review*, vol.83, Feb. 1938, p.90.

24. *Architectural Review*, vol.77, Jan. 1935, caption to plate iv.

25. *Building News*, vol 7, 22 Mar. 1861, p.252.

26. 'Bliss Was It in That Dawn to Be Alive': an Interview with John Brandon-Jones', *Architectural Design*, vol.49, no.10/11, 1979, p.98.

raphy modern architecture could never have been "put across"'.[27] While Shand's enthusiasm for this holy alliance was not universally shared, even as hostile a critic as Sir Reginald Blomfield could not deny the photograph's power. Blomfield not only wrote that he thought 'that the illustrations of old buildings in our weekly journals are largely responsible for the revolt of the New Architecture',[28] he also admitted that the growth of the Modern Movement had been accomplished largely by photography –

> It has spread to this country and is now widely advertised as the one and only gospel of artistic salvation. Large compilations of photographs are constantly being published, and let loose on an unsuspecting public, and the traditionalists are so content with their ways, or so immersed in their multifarious works, that some fine day they may find their foundations undermined, and themselves buried under the ruins of what they had assumed to be an assured position.[29]

Blomfield was right to be worried. These enticing photographs continue to slew our judgments today, giving the false impression that modernism dominated the architectural output of the period rather than accounting for a small fraction of it. Just as the devil had the best tunes, so modernism had the best, most captivating photographs. A Bedford Lemere study of one of the many classical town halls built during the 1930s simply does not leap off the page with the same compelling power as a dynamically vigorous image by Dell and Wainwright. Indeed it was a contemporary joke that the importance of photography was so great that 'the modern school of architects ... designed their buildings not to please their clients or even themselves, but to please Dell and Wainwright'.[30]

Others joined Blomfield in condemnation of the influence wielded by the Dell and Wainwright school of architectural photography. In a radio talk broadcast in 1961 C. Fleetwood-Walker condemned its pernicious effect on British architecture and even Jim Richards, looking back in his autobiography, admitted, 'They flattered the buildings they photographed to a degree that delighted architects but caused me some misgivings.'[31] Perhaps the most provocative criticism came in the artist Michael Rothenstein's article 'Colour and Modern Architecture or the Photographic Eye'[32] published in the *Architectural Review* in 1946, in which he argued that modern architecture had degenerated into a colourless idiom largely because of the ubiquity of seductive black-and-white photographs. Thus Rothenstein condemned architectural photographs as misleading

> for they so often show us walls and window-openings bathed in clear sunlight. The relationship between different volumes is thus shown to great advantage; while in the cloudy light typical of our own weather, cast shadows rarely lend such vigorous character to the contrasting planes. The modern architect imitates the photographer; he builds with lights and shadows, with black and white. The infinitely varied polychromatic possibilities of his medium are neglected. The great majority of modern buildings are conceived in an uninteresting chiaroscuro, an empty scheme of lights and half-tones which rely upon the window-openings to afford relief.[33]

Ironically, although Rothenstein did not say so, many early modernist buildings such as Le Corbusier's Villa Savoye were in fact highly coloured and magazines were certainly guilty (though not as much as is often supposed) of using a variety of retouching techniques, including the application of whitener, to accentuate their supposedly monochromatic qualities. A good example is Felton's photograph published in the *Architectural Review* in 1933 of Connell, Ward and Lucas's Alding, Grayswood, where the light pink walls were deliberately blanched.

Despite these criticisms the Dell and Wainwright style remained the norm

Figure 22. Dell & Wainwright. Midland Hotel, Morecambe (1933). Architect: Oliver Hill (Architectural Press Archive / RIBA Library Photographs Collection).

27. *Architectural Review*, vol.75, Jan. 1934, p.12.

28. Sir Reginald Blomfield, *Modernismus*, London, Macmillan, 1934, p.69.

29. ibid., pp.51–52

30. *Architects' Journal*, vol.106, 13 June 1946, p.445.

31. J M Richards, *Memoirs of an Unjust Fella*, London, Weidenfeld & Nicholson, 1980, p.137.

32. Michael Rothenstein, 'Colour and Modern Architecture or the Photographic Eye', *Architectural Review*, vol.99, June 1946, pp.159–163.

33. *Architectural Review*, vol.99, June 1946, pp.159–160.

34. Quoted in 'Bliss Was It in That Dawn
to Be Alive', p.98.

in British architectural photography, influencing the work of post-war practitioners such as Henk Snoek and Richard Einzig. This influence was also felt abroad with the great American architectural photographer Ezra Stoller confessing his admiration and debt. It was only in the 1960s that a serious challenge to this prevailing orthodoxy was mounted with the espousal of the photojournalistic approach seen in the work of John Donat and Tony Ray-Jones who used 35mm cameras to capture pictures of buildings in use. Ironically since then the rise of colour photography, with the relatively slow speed of large format films, has seen a reversion to the formal abstraction associated with the *Architectural Review*'s duo.

Today photographs dominate architectural discourse but that dominance is increasingly being attacked with resounding denunciations of the architectural photograph's perceived flattering mendacity; its insatiable fetish for details that prizes striking pictures over architectural revelation; and its stubborn neglect of the way buildings are used and perform over time. As we have seen, however, there is nothing new in such criticisms for it was during the inter-war years that the camera firmly established its supremacy in architectural recording and contemporaries were alive to the dangers this presented. Since then these dangers have increased not only with the added glamorous allure of colour but more importantly with a major shift in patronage which has seen magazines commission less photography and consequently become more reliant on photographs paid for and supplied by the architects of the buildings to be published. The result is that the ironically perceptive observation made in the 1930s by Goodhart-Rendel, President of the RIBA, has greater resonance than ever – 'The modern architectural drawing is interesting, the photograph is magnificent, the building is an unfortunate but necessary stage between the two.'[34]

4 SCHOOL DESIGN IN THE 1930S

DENIS CLARKE HALL

SCHOOL DESIGN IN THE 1930S

DENIS CLARKE HALL

Sadly, there are now very few of us left who actually practised in the 1930s, so I would like to try to give something of the atmosphere of that time. The 1930s were considered by many as a terrible period. There was the slump, vast unemployment, terrible poverty, the rise of Nazism, Fascism and the Spanish Civil War. But there was also an incredible surge of new thought and ideas in practically every aspect of civil life. Engineers were developing new ships, aeroplanes and cars. The arts were an inspiration. Picasso and Braque were at work and I remember Henry Moore's first exhibition at the Lefevre Gallery when he was struggling to overcome intense opposition.

To a young student at the Architectural Association it was very exciting to discover all these things. To me they were particularly exciting: in 1937 I had just got married, had my first child and I had won £500 in a competition. That was an absolute fortune; I had been living on £2 a week. On top of that, within a month I had been commissioned to build a school in Yorkshire.

It was a period of great discussions. I remember going to the Café Royal night after night; the old Café Royal with its marble-topped tables and plush chairs. We would sit there over a coffee all evening. If you wanted something to eat, you got a sandwich. Those were times that felt unique.

There was an extraordinary jumble of architectural styles. I had gone through the AA looking at all sorts of traditional styles, while searching for something that really meant something to a young person. Then I discovered the Modern Movement with its traditional classic proportions, pure logic and beautiful use of form in relation to windows. It was an absolute revelation and it altered the whole of one's attitude towards architecture.

In 1926, the Hadow Report came out with new ideas on education. Before that there was a mixture of small Board Schools dotted all over the country. The Report suggested that, at the age of 11, children should go on to senior elementary schools. The Report was followed by many others but implementation of its ideas was very slow. In the early 1930s there was no money because of the slump. By the middle 1930s there was a great surge of education buildings to accommodate these new secondary pupils. Many architects were working on them, including Maxwell Fry at Impington, C. G. Stillman with his schools in Sussex; it was all beginning to build up to the great climax that came after the war.

In the middle of this Professor Reilly of Liverpool persuaded Gerald Barry at the *News Chronicle* to run a competition for an ideal school. The competition was in two sections: one for a senior elementary school in an urban setting for 460 11–14 year olds; the other one was a small rural school for around 150 pupils.

I entered the competition having just qualified. In those days you had to do six months' practical experience before you qualified. I worked with Clive Entwistle. He was an extraordinary man who had worked with Le Corbusier. He had a little studio flat cum office at the top of a building over the Walker Galleries in Bond Street. I learned absolutely nothing about professional practice but we did have wonderful discussions about architecture. As soon as I left

Figure 1. The Gymnasium, Richmond Girls High School, in c.1940

Figure 2. Denis Clarke Hall on winning the *News Chronicle* schools competition in March 1937.

him the *News Chronicle* competition was announced. I soon realised that I knew absolutely nothing at all about school buildings. We were given three months to design the building and enter our schemes. I spent most of that time researching the requirements of a school. This resulted in a four and a half page article in the *Architects' Journal*. The article was divided into four parts: first, the requirements of a school; second, the application to a building; third, a description of the building; and fourth, construction and costs. The report, rather than the design of the building, won me the competition. After that I was commissioned within a month to build a school in Yorkshire.

So there was I knowing nothing about professional practices but with £500 and a commission. I set up office in Sackville Street. At that time, local authorities would not employ engineers or quantity surveyors; architects had to do the lot. I could not understand how I was going to build a modern building without an engineer. I knew Ove Arup from the AA when he used to visit and go round telling students about their designs. I used to follow him around and absorb

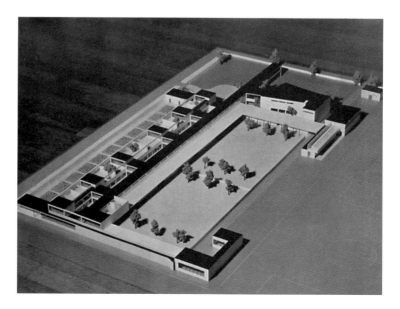

Figure 3. Model of the *News Chronicle* winning design, 1937.

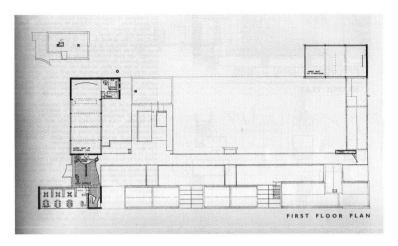

FIRST FLOOR PLAN

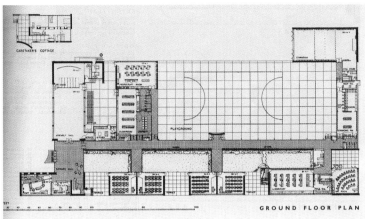

GROUND FLOOR PLAN

Figure 4. Plans of Richmond Girls High School, 1937–8.

everything he had to say. I went and saw him and asked what I should do about the engineering side of the building. He was working with J. L. Kier and Company at the time and said that he was just about to leave and start his own office. He said that he had an engineer whom he wanted to employ but that he had nothing for him just then. The suggestion was that I took him into my office, paid his salary and the engineering would be taken care of. I had Arup for the price of paying his assistant's salary. I also wanted quantity surveyors. Owen Davis of Davis and Bellfield had just qualified and had no office. He took over the job at a bargain rate. Then a young man of about sixteen rang my doorbell and said that Eric Brown of the Kingston School of Architecture had sent him, thinking that I might give him a job. He said he could draw, and he produced the most beautiful drawings. He turned out to be Nick Montgomery, later of Montgomery, Alfield and Kirby, a firm which worked in Africa.

Then I went to Yorkshire to see Richmond. Richmond is a beautiful traditional town in the middle of the most marvellous country and there was I, hoping to put a modern building in it. It was a mainly stone town and I came to the conclusion that I had to use local stone. The result was load-bearing walls of local stone right down to the foundations with everything that was in stress designed by Arup's in concrete.

The local authority really objected strongly to the idea of a modern school in their town. But the Education Officer, Frank Barraclough, was a real patron to me. First, he was the person who selected me from the six architects whom the RIBA recommended to the North Riding, and then he helped push through the planning decisions. The Chief Architect to the Board of Education had to go all

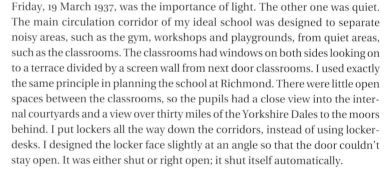

Figure 5. Richmond Girls High School on completion in 1940, south-facing classroom range.

Figure 6. Richmond Girls High School under construction in 1938–9.

the way up to Richmond to persuade the local authority to build the school.

One of the key things that came out in my report to the *News Chronicle* of Friday, 19 March 1937, was the importance of light. The other one was quiet. The main circulation corridor of my ideal school was designed to separate noisy areas, such as the gym, workshops and playgrounds, from quiet areas, such as the classrooms. The classrooms had windows on both sides looking on to a terrace divided by a screen wall from next door classrooms. I used exactly the same principle in planning the school at Richmond. There were little open spaces between the classrooms, so the pupils had a close view into the internal courtyards and a view over thirty miles of the Yorkshire Dales to the moors behind. I put lockers all the way down the corridors, instead of using locker-desks. I designed the locker face slightly at an angle so that the door couldn't stay open. It was either shut or right open; it shut itself automatically.

The stone construction had to be taken right down to the foundations so that you could really see its solidity. Portal frames and infill panels were in reinforced concrete. Little windows for the lavatories and staff rooms looked like holes in a solid stone wall. The freestanding chimney was known as the phallus of Richmond. It was constructed of concrete drainpipes around an internal lining of firebricks and with reinforced concrete in between. The concrete used in the canopy over the main entrance was very thin indeed. The canopy is three inches thick. One day, I was talking to Barraclough and said I would show him what concrete would do. So I took him out on that canopy and jumped. The concrete canopy went up and down like a springboard. I have never seen anybody move so quickly. I had learned a lot about concrete when doing my thesis at the AA. Howard Robertson was the Principal and I used to have to go to him very Friday and discuss concrete designs and finishes. I remember seeing Eugène Mopin, who had just been commissioned to do the Quarry Hill flats in Leeds (demolished in 1978), demonstrating vibrated concrete panels in a steel mould at the Building Centre, which was then in Bond Street. I watched him mixing up the concrete himself, pouring it on a steel mould, putting it on a vibrator, leaving it there for two or three minutes, turning it upside down and there was a marvellous copy of the mould without a crumble coming off it.

School furniture in those days was just heavy cast iron frames holding up solid oak desks and seats. I could not find anything that I wanted to go into my building and so I persuaded the authorities to let me design the furniture. The result was that I designed every piece of furniture in the school except in the staff rooms where the furniture had to be upholstered. I wanted to use nesting furniture and at that time there were two patents, one held by PEL and one designed by Aalto for Finmar. I approached PEL, who would have nothing to do with me, while Finmar said I had to get permission from Aalto. I wrote to Aalto and nothing happened, until finally I got a telegram: 'Approved. Negotiate with Finmar.' The telegram had come from Aalto while he was fighting at the front in the Russo-Finnish War.

The assembly hall, which had tip-up seats, doubled as the dining room. The tables were designed with runners to slide in under the stage. There was also a small projection room at the back. The screen slid back into the corridor through a little trap door allowing the entrance hall to be opened up to the main assembly hall. There was stage lighting as well since the hall was designed to be used by the local community as well as by the school; another feature which came out of my research.

Another finding that I made while doing my research into schools was that

[Clockwise from top right]

Figure 7. Entrance hall at Richmond Girls High School in 1940.

Figure 8. Staff room, with Finmar furniture designed by Alvar Aalto.

Figure 9. Assembly hall, with its tip-up, stackable seats.

there was a problem with glare on traditional blackboards. The right combination to use for maximum visibility was pale primrose yellow blackboards with a deep royal blue chalk. I persuaded the local authority to have all the blackboards yellow with blue chalk but only if I painted the boards black on the other side so that if the teachers did not like it they could reverse them. The trouble was that the blue chalk came off all over the teachers' dresses. So most of the blackboards went back to being black – except in the laboratory where the teacher changed her dresses instead.

In those days all schools had chocolate brown paint and dark green walls and old worn wooden floors. I persuaded the local authority to change all that and I managed to get them to accept blue quarry tile floors and white paint. The paint was criticised because it would get so dirty. I said it would not get any dirtier than brown paint. You would see the dirt more and so the walls might be cleaned more often. I visited the school about six years after it was completed, after the war, and the white paint was immaculate. I asked the headmistress how she managed to keep it so clean. She said the pupils took such a pride in the building that no one was allowed to make any mess. If they did, they cleaned it up themselves. I thought that was quite an achievement.

The war came and I had not finished the school. There were awful rumours that it was going to be turned into an air raid shelter, and the Kiefer windows were stuck on the continent somewhere. We finally got them across, badly damaged, but they were marvellous Swiss windows. They are made of such fine wood that the glazing bars and frames could be kept really thin. Little wedges were tapped into the corner of the glass sheets to keep the windows absolutely square.

After the war, England was absolutely devastated. All our major cities and all commercial centres had been bombed and burned out. Tens of thousands of houses had been demolished or badly damaged and the Butler Act of 1944 made pretty well every school in the country out-of-date. Stillman, who quickly became the County Architect of Middlesex, asked me to go round his schools to do a report on whether they came up to the Butler Act's requirements. I could not find one that did.

Conditions after the war were very different. I had done what I thought was a good, interesting scheme for an infants' school in Ormsby in Yorkshire which was commissioned before the war, a year after I started on Richmond. But in 1946 I was told to get on with a new commission. Now there were no materials and no labour. The shortage of materials was acute; you never knew what you were going to get. But I still tried to keep to the same principles of separation of noisy areas from quiet areas by the circulation spaces. Instead of a concrete framework, we used trusses for the assembly hall, built up with reinforcing

Figure 10. Caretaker's cottage, showing the mix of modern and traditional materials at Richmond Girls High School.

Figure 11. Richmond Secondary Modern School, built next to the High School in 1957–9. They are now one comprehensive school.

rods and anything we could get hold of. This was due entirely to economy, not to a change of ideas on my part.

I was also commissioned to design a six-form entry school in Essex. It was enormous. I tried to stick to the same principles of isolated classrooms but it would have taken the headmaster twenty minutes to go from his room around to every other room. I worked on a very tight site for Stillman at Cranford in Middlesex and produced a simple tight block. And I added a secondary modern to the Richmond school for another 600 pupils. This was built sticking straight out of the hill, with a two-storey end running into a four-storey block at the bottom of the hill.

ENDNOTE BY ELAIN HARWOOD

Denis Clarke Hall (1910–2006) went on to design schools across England and Wales, until ill-health forced his retirement in the 1970s. Although he built 27 schools for eleven local authorities and became one of this country's leading authorities on school design, it is arguable whether any repeated the acclaim accorded his first school at Richmond. Moreover, as he himself has suggested, the three radical elements of school design which he introduced with his competition entry – the use of prefabricated materials, the relaxed plan and the attention given to natural daylight – came each in turn to be abandoned in the 1950s.

By the time that Richmond was under construction, Clarke Hall had turned his scientific mind to prefabrication. He produced a report in 1938 on the application of production methods to housing that led to his joining the Committee for the Industrial and Scientific Provision of Housing founded by Harry Weston, Chairman of Coventry City Council. He was also one of two architect members of the Wood Committee set up by the Ministry of Education in 1943 to consider standardised construction and to advise on planning and layouts for the new schools needed after the war.[1] But in reality, as Clarke Hall said in

1. R. B. White, Prefabrication, London, HMSO, 1965, pp.125, 225.

2. Denis Clarke Hall in conversation, 18 January 2006.

3. Denis Clarke Hall, 'Secondary Schools', in *Architect and Building News*, vol.192, no.4115, 31 October 1947, p.98.

his last interviews, it proved just too difficult to get all the contractors to deliver their components to a site at the right moment, and from the late 1940s he returned to conventional brick and concrete construction.

Clarke Hall explains at the end of his article that the need to build very large schools, particularly for secondary education, made loose planning difficult. A still more serious problem was the strict economy with which schools had to be built in the post-war years. Having devalued the pound in September 1949, Stafford Cripps cut the civil capital expenditure programme by £150 million. For 1950 there was to be a maximum of £170 per place for primary schools and £290 for secondary schools, reduced for 1951 to £140 and £240 respectively. His Conservative successors kept these figures almost static despite a rise in builders' costs once controls on materials were lifted in 1954, estimated by Middlesex CC at 16%. This had a serious impact on school design; Denis Clarke Hall recalled how he, the County Architect and Deputy Architect for the North Riding were summoned to London to show high-ranking Ministers how they could lop an overspend of just £3,000 off the cost of a school.[2] Economies were commonly made by reducing circulation space to a minimum, and by incorporating dining room facilities within assembly halls. The contrast between the Richmond Girls High School and the post-war Secondary Modern on the adjoining site could not be greater: all the accommodation in the 1950s school is in a single slab built into the side of the hill, with laboratories and classrooms stacked in two rows over the assembly hall and gymnasium.

Of greater lasting influence was Clarke Hall's pioneering work on daylighting. The Ministry of Education in 1945 reconfigured Clarke Hall's 'foot candle' measurements as a 'daylight factor' of two per cent, the proportion of light received at a given spot indoors from an unobstructed hemisphere of uniformly bright sky. This percentage was usually only attainable by having windows on both sides of the classroom.[3] Revised regulations in 1951 accepted that natural lighting was but one factor in a school's design, and while daylighting remained the single greatest determinant of post-war school design until c.1970, more multi-storey schools began to be built. It was his special interest in top-lighting that led Clarke Hall to be commissioned to produce a standard plan for Middlesex CC, and it remained a feature of his work. This interest is well seen in the complex lightwells at the large secondary moderns like Richmond and The Riddings, Scunthorpe, another slab-like Secondary Modern and built with his partner Sam Scorer in 1958.

The post-war schools designed by Denis Clarke Hall range from tiny primaries to multi-storey secondary schools. The primary schools include Ormesby (1946) and Cherry Orchard in Greenwich (1950), while Richmond (1957–9), Coalville (1958–62) and Kenfig in Glamorgan (1959) are perhaps the best of his surviving secondary moderns (all are now comprehensive schools). His most famous post-war secondary school was that at Cranford, Middlesex, which in 1950–3 introduced a strikingly compact and economical square plan that was very different from the Richmond Girls' High School; unfortunately it was on the flight path into Heathrow and was closed in 1985 because of the noise. Clarke Hall was also the assessor for the Hunstanton School competition won by Alison and Peter Smithson and, against strong local opposition, championed the building of their economical but rigidly symmetrical design.

Denis Clarke Hall's extensive work outside the realm of schools included the entrance to the Homes and Gardens Pavilion at the Festival of Britain in 1951 – one of the few consciously temporary buildings for the exhibition, being made entirely of canvas. He also produced public housing for Hornchurch and St Pancras Councils, and civic centres at Egham, Surrey, and Cranbrook, Kent, the latter of particular interest as he had again to relate a modern building to a historic setting. Clarke Hall never again entered a competition, however, and he was proud that he secured ample work by direct commissions.

5 THE LIFE AND WORK OF SIR OWEN WILLIAMS 1890–1969

ROYSTON FOOT

THE LIFE AND WORK OF
SIR OWEN WILLIAMS 1890–1969

ROYSTON FOOT

S ir Owen Williams was born in London on 20 March 1890. His father and mother both came from north Wales and his father ran a grocer's shop in north London. Owen attended Tottenham Grammar School, from which he matriculated in 1906.

On leaving school Williams joined the Metropolitan Electric Tramway Company as an apprentice and at the same time he enrolled in the Northern Polytechnic to study engineering at evening classes. In 1911 he gained his BSc, from London University, sitting as an external student and obtaining first class honours. A short while later he was also awarded the City & Guilds Institute's Silver Medal in Structural Engineering – the highest award of that institute.

After graduating, no doubt wishing to enlarge his experience, he left the Tramway Company and worked first for the Indented Bar & Concrete Company before moving on again to the Trussed Concrete Steel Company.

More than 90 years ago the use of reinforced concrete was very much in its infancy in Britain and Sir Owen was in at the birth, working on an enormous range of concrete projects. He was not only a vastly experienced exponent of its design properties, but also a passionate and eloquent advocate of its design potential, to the extent that his nickname in the papers – and he was always a great letter-writer to the papers – was 'Concrete Williams'.

During the First World War Sir Owen worked on projects connected with the war. Somewhat surprisingly, he seemed to become disenchanted with civil engineering, even though by this time he was a member of the Institution of Civil Engineers. He became a Fellow of the Aeronautical Society of Great Britain, and then worked as the chief designer for the Wells Aviation Company on the design for a seaplane. However, that phase passed and he was seconded to

Figure 1. Daily Express, Fleet Street, London, 1929–31, Sir Owen Williams with H. O. Ellis and Clarke.

Figure 1. Owen Williams in the early 1920s.

the Admiralty where he worked on the design of concrete ships, becoming an Associate Member of the Institution of Naval Architects into the bargain.

Thus, during his career, this remarkable man practised as a civil engineer – becoming one of a very small band to gain two Telford Gold Medals from the Institution of Civil Engineers, the highest award it can bestow upon a member; as an aeronautical engineer; as a naval architect; and as an architect who, as we shall see, was responsible for some of the landmark buildings of the 1920s and 1930s.

Following the end of the war, Sir Owen started his own consultancy practice in 1919. He worked mainly on industrial buildings, using his skill in reinforced concrete to overcome the shortage of more traditional materials that had resulted from the war. However, the major impetus to his career came with his appointment as the consulting engineer to the Empire Exhibition at Wembley where he worked alongside the architects Simpson & Ayrton.

The project caught the public's interest, the papers of the day made a great fuss of the use of this new material, reinforced concrete, and Williams continued to be a fluent and compelling advocate for its use. King George V opened the exhibition in April 1924 and it went on to attract widespread interest and publicity both for its architects and its engineer. John Simpson and Owen Williams were each rewarded with knighthoods, a fitting acknowledgement for the enormous amount of work they had put in during the previous three years. Thus, at the age of 34, 'Concrete Williams' had become Sir Owen Williams.

After the success of the exhibition, Sir Owen became very much involved in the design of bridges. He worked mainly with Maxwell Ayrton, who acted as the architect, and probably the greatest number of the bridges that remain are to be found in Scotland on what is now the A90. However, towards the end of the 1920s it appears that Sir Owen increasingly wished to be free of the restraints of working with architects, and to have the freedom to work on his own.

To some degree he achieved this with his appointment to work with Sir

Figure 2. Palace of Engineering, Wembley Exhibition, 1923–4, demolished.

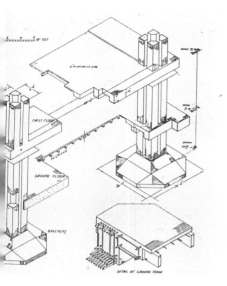

Robert McAlpine on the Dorchester Hotel. The story of the development of the hotel is somewhat complicated, but I think that now all would agree that its design is very much down to Williams.

The next major project on which Sir Owen worked was also somewhat controversial. This was the *Daily Express* building in London's Fleet Street. Sir Owen told me that his involvement sprang from a lunch-time meeting with Lord Beaverbrook. Apparently Beaverbrook was concerned that the building that was then under construction would not provide the working space around his new presses that he felt was necessary. He asked Sir Owen if he would have a look at the building to see if he could improve matters.

Sir Owen did so and next afternoon came up with a structural design that provided a clear span of some 58'6" in the press hall, sufficient to house the three eight-foot-wide presses, with ten feet of working space between them and six feet clearance on each side. Sir Owen was appointed to take over the project but did so only on the understanding that the original architects were retained, to which the *Express* agreed. However, if the structural design was the basic reason for Sir Owen's appointment, the black glass of the elevation caught the attention of the architectural press and the public. There has been discussion over the years about whose idea this was, but I believe Sir Owen, who always maintained that it was his, and having seen the design by the original architects for the elevation, I think it inconceivable that they would have put forward such a radical alteration. Certainly both the other *Daily Express* buildings that Sir Owen did in Manchester and Glasgow had the familiar black glass treatment of the elevation.

There was no controversy over Sir Owen's next project, which was the first where he was without doubt both architect and engineer: the Boots Wets Building (D10) in Nottingham. This is the building, perhaps above all others, that has firmly established his reputation as a major figure in modern British architecture.

At the time of his appointment in 1930, Boots was an American-owned company, the United Drugs Company of America, which intended to construct a huge industrial complex on the 300-acre site that it had acquired in the late 1920s in Nottingham. The company's aim was to manufacture their so-called Wets and Drys products on one site. Work began first on the Wets Building, but did not start on the Drys Building for another five or so years by which time the Boots company had once again reverted to British ownership.

Figure 4. Detail of reinforced concrete frame construction, Dorchester Hotel.

Figure 3. Perspective of Williams's scheme for the Dorchester Hotel, Park Lane, London, 1930.

Figure 5. Boots Packed Wet Goods Building (D10), Beeston, Notts, 1931–2, under construction.

Figure 6. The interior of the Wets Building under construction in 1931.

Figure 7. Sainsbury's factory and warehouse, Paris Garden, Southwark, 1931–3.

On completion, the D10 factory made a considerable impact on the architectural press. It was hailed as an example of functionalist architecture never before achieved in this country. Sir Owen would not have been impressed! He was never happy to be connected with any group – he wanted to be his own man. If a client approached him to undertake a commission, he discussed it in detail with him and then settled down to give that client the best circumstances that he, Sir Owen Williams, could achieve. That was his philosophy. It was also a *sine qua non* that the resulting building should be constructed as efficiently and as economically as possible, as had been the case with the Boots building. As he was fond of saying, it was all done for 'ten bob a square foot' – not a bad bargain!

Sir Owen's reputation stood high after Boots, and his output was impressive. The Cumberland Garage at Marble Arch – the capital's first multi-storey garage – the Dollis Hill Synagogue, laboratories for Tunnel Cement, flats in Stanmore and a factory for Sainsbury's in Stamford Street in Blackfriars were all achieved with a staff of never more than a couple of dozen, himself and his secretary included. From this prolific period there are several other landmark buildings: the Empire Pool at Wembley, Peckham's Pioneer Health Centre, the Boots Drys Building, and the *Daily Express* buildings in Manchester and Glasgow.

The Empire Pool commission sprang from his friendship with Sir Arthur

Elvin. Elvin had run a tobacco kiosk at the Empire Exhibition and had gone on to acquire the buildings after the closure of the exhibition, leasing them out to a variety of businesses. However, it was his work as the Chief Executive of Wembley Stadium Trust which brought him his knighthood, as it was very much his drive and energy that led to the stadium being recognised worldwide as the home of international football. So it was Elvin who commissioned the Empire Pool to be ready in time for the 1934 Empire Games.

The pool was built on the old exhibition site and, at the time of its construction, its owners proudly boasted that it was the largest swimming pool in the world: 60' wide and 200' long. The building itself, structurally a series of three pinned arches, has clear spans of 230' without any visual or structural obstructions for the spectators. If this were not enough, the whole construction time from the start to the official opening by the Duke of Gloucester was only nine months. Interestingly too, the building illustrates Sir Owen's carefully considered modular approach to the design of his buildings. The Middlesex County Council Building Regulations stipulated that terrace stairs should have a rise of six inches and a going, or tread, of eleven inches. So the vertical module for the entire building is three feet – six times six inches – and the horizontal module is two feet nine inches: three times eleven inches.

The Pioneer Health Centre at Peckham was constructed as a result of the work of two doctors. For some years Dr Innes Pearse and Dr Scott Williamson had been carrying out a pilot study whereby families could receive medical checks on a regular basis, while at the same time being encouraged to take part in healthy recreation, all at the cost of one shilling per week. The work was supported financially by J. Donaldson. In 1933 it was felt that results were strong enough for them to carry out a much larger and longer-term study, provided the cost of constructing the necessary centre could be kept below £25,000.

Their approach to various architects asking for design proposals but stipulating a ceiling cost of £25,000 caused something of a rumpus, with charges from one of the architects approached that the RIBA's rules on professional conduct had been breached. Sir Owen's direct appointment settled concerns over that, and probably came about through his connections with the

Clockwise from top right

Figure 8. Owen Williams (with pencil) and the Prince of Wales (at left, with scarf) discussing a detail of the Empire Pool in 1934. Sir Arthur Elvin is in the group to the rear.

Figure 9. Empire Pool, Wembley, 1933–4, now Wembley Arena, with the Palaces of Art, Industry and Engineering from 1923–4 in a receding line to the left.

Figure 10. Interior of the Empire Pool, the pool half covered over.

Figure 11. Pioneer Health Centre, Peckham, 1933–5, by night.

Figure 12. The same view by day.

Sainsbury family. He did the job most successfully, once again using his favourite flat-slab construction. Perhaps the closing sentence of the assessment published at the time in the *Architectural Review* gives a worthy epitaph: "This building is architecturally alive and no crudity of execution can destroy that vitality – any more than elaborate consideration of detail can bring a dead building to life."

The Drys Building at Boots was another major building of the mid-to late 1930s. Although the original intention had been to make the Wets and Drys Buildings mirror the forms of each other, much had changed in the four or five years between their construction. The American company had relinquished ownership of Boots back to the English family, and the latter's ideas of manufacturing no doubt influenced the fundamental change in the design of the two buildings. Like the first building, the Drys is huge, but the manufacturing process is virtually reversed from that of the Wets. Whereas in the Wets Building raw materials go by chute to the ground floor for manufacture, in the Drys they went by lift to the top floor for manufacture and the finished products were transferred by chute back to the ground floor.

The construction too is different in some important respects. Over the single-storey sections – which incidentally have huge cantilevers over the loading and unloading docks. The ends of the beams over these single-storey parts are supported by hangers, which in turn are carried on the very deep beams above roof level. The hangers give a very strong vertical emphasis to the elevation yet they also have a practical function. They are hollow concrete boxes and serve as the extraction ducts for the building, each hanger having a large fan at roof level to aid the extraction.

Towards the end of the 1930s, two further buildings for Express Newspapers were completed, one in Manchester and one in Glasgow. The Glasgow building is the less interesting of the two from an architectural point of view. I remember it for the fact that unlike the other Express buildings, where the printing presses were located in the basement, in Glasgow they were positioned on the ground floor. The consequent design loading was a quarter of a ton per square foot and when I worked on the post-war extension this was the heaviest design loading I ever used anywhere.

The *Daily Express* building in Manchester again gave Sir Owen the chance to use his much-favoured flat-slab construction, supported on cruciform columns. It had to be built in such a way that production of the paper could continue in the old building while the new one was built around it. It was further complicated by the fact that the owner of the Whittakers furniture store, which was at the corner of the building on the main Ancoats Street frontage, thought he could make his fortune by holding out for a large sum of money to give up his premises. In the event, the building was put up around him and he was just left to carry on his business.

One of the most interesting aspects of the building, which was erected before World War II, was its false floor. By the time he was working on the building, Sir Owen had long realised that newspaper office layouts were always being altered. This meant disruption while telephone wires and cables, lighting cables and the rest were somehow re-routed to new positions. To overcome this problem, he designed a false floor of thick plywood panels, each three feet square, with a topping of thick industrial linoleum. These panels were supported at their four corners by adjustable metal pillars some three inches high that could be levelled accurately to give a flat surface. The great virtue of the floor was that it could be taken up very quickly, the alterations to cabling and telephones made rapidly, and the whole put back in position with the minimum of disruption.

Other buildings, of course, were constructed during what may be thought of as Sir Owen's golden period, but I have mentioned those that are probably most noteworthy. War came soon after completion of the Manchester *Daily Express* and Sir Owen again became deeply involved with concrete ships. After the war, he undertook one of his best but perhaps least known projects, the magnificent maintenance hangars for the British Overseas Airways Corporation (later British Airways) at London Airport, as well as major extensions to the *Express* buildings at Glasgow and Manchester. His last major building before he turned all of his attention to motorways was the *Daily Mirror* building at Holborn.

His health began to deteriorate in the mid-1960s and he relinquished control of his practice to his son, O.T. Williams. He suffered a stroke in the spring of 1969 and died shortly thereafter, on 23 May, at the age of 79.

Sir Owen Williams was a remarkable man. He was a man of ideas and he was never afraid to put them forward. He was an inveterate writer of letters to

Figure 13. Boots Dry Goods Building (D6), Beeston, Notts, 1935–8. The unloading of the materials for making pills and lozenges is undertaken in the low building, then they are manufactured and packed using a system of lifts and chutes in the tall one. The building is now offices.

Figure 14. Owen Williams in the 1960s.

The Times. He wrote numerous articles and papers and he was an articulate and persuasive advocate for his wide-ranging ideas and beliefs. Above all, however, he had supreme confidence in his ability as an engineer and in his use of reinforced concrete as the structural medium to achieve his engineering solutions. It was from that confidence and that engineering ability that his landmark architecture sprang.

6 REDISCOVERING LUBETKIN

JOHN ALLAN

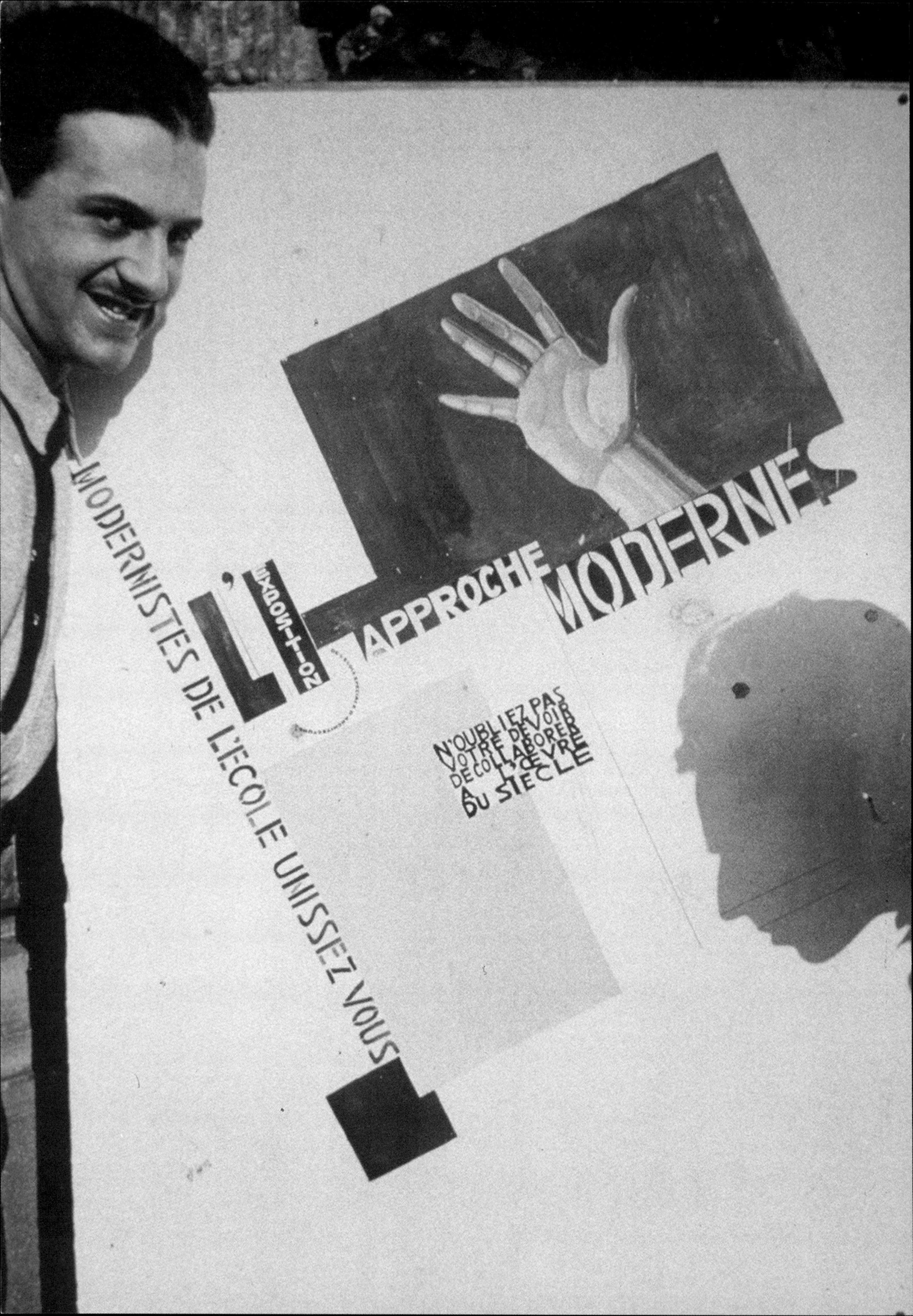
MODERNISTES DE L'ECOLE UNISSEZ VOUS
L' EXPOSITION APPROCHE MODERNES
N'OUBLIEZ PAS
VOTRE DEVOIR
DE COLLABORER
A L'ŒUVRE
DU SIECLE

REDISCOVERING LUBETKIN

JOHN ALLAN

At two important moments in 20th century architectural discourse we have, with unfortunate consequences, allowed Americans to codify the position and direction of the European Modern Movement. The first occasion was 1932 when Henry-Russell Hitchcock and Philip Johnson's study *The International Style*[1] imposed a specious singularity on the various manifestations of exploratory thought and design that in most European countries were still in a molten state, albeit beginning to show signs of local crusting. The second occasion was in 1966 when Robert Venturi's essay 'Complexity and Contradiction in Architecture'[2] employed a similar sort of generalisation in order to distinguish modernist aspirations from those of almost every other period or style in architectural history.

These respective dates, 1932 and 1966, which fortuitously coincide with the beginning and end of Berthold Lubetkin's professional career in England, might be regarded as defining the time frame within which his work is commonly interpreted. And both of the above-mentioned books, or rather the theses they promoted, helped to establish popular historical orthodoxies which I feel have diminished or distorted a full appreciation of Lubetkin's work and ideas. The first gave primacy to an apparent stylistic and programmatic consistency to the exclusion or detriment of other more complex themes: irony, metaphor, the exotic, the role of history; the second suggested that because such subtleties supposedly neither had been, nor could be, accommodated by modern architecture, a whole other architectural value-system was needed.

Conscious as I am of the risk of perpetrating an equivalent form of oversimplification, I nevertheless propose to address these problematic aspects of Lubetkin's artistic personality which tend to be either criticised or neglected as a result of the historiographic template reinforced by books such as the above.

By saying little about those issues that usually feature prominently in discussions of Lubetkin – his Socialism and the interaction of his political and professional agendas – I do not intend to downplay these crucial aspects of his story. I simply wish to focus on something else in this particular essay – that is, his *artistic* sources and their vital inspirational and polemical role in his work. To help appreciate this, some initial contextualisation might be helpful.

It is not necessary to make a straw man of Functionalism to differentiate Lubetkin's anomalous position in the context of inter-war British modernism. But precisely because he was such a key figure in its 'heroic period' his critical reputation began to suffer when his own work transgressed the received canon it had helped to establish. The fact that Lubetkin was a *second generation* modernist, being born some 15 years later than the 'founding fathers', Corbu, Mies et al., does not mean that his vision of modern architecture was *second hand*, or that he did not have his own vital and perhaps unique blend of formative influences.

On the contrary, in his case, an incredibly rapid mastery of modern architecture's new technical toolbox only hastened the moment when he was ready to give it his own spin. Not only was his 'professional education' as unconventional

Figure 1. Modernists Unite. Berthold Lubetkin as a student at the Ecole Speciale d'Architecture, Paris, 1925.

1. H.R. Hitchcock & P. Johnson, *The International Style*, New York, Museum of Modern Art, 1932.

2. R. Venturi, *Complexity and Contradiction in Architecture*, New York, Museum of Modern Art, 1966.

Figure 2. Apartment block, 25 Avenue de Versailles, Paris. Completed in 1931 by Lubetkin and Jean Ginsburg contemporaneously with Villa Savoye, when they were still in their 20s. (Photo Studio Jyska).

3. R. Banham, *Theory and Design in the First Machine Age*, London, Architectural Press, 1960, p.321.

4. B. Lubetkin, 'Modern Architecture in England', *American Architect and Architecture*, vol. 150. February 1937, pp. 29–30.

as it is possible to imagine (yielding no formal qualifications whatever), his early life in revolutionary Russia and the extraordinary auto-didactic decade spent reaching England via Germany, Austria, Poland and France, with all its fabulous exploits and encounters, had equipped him with resources of historical knowledge, imaginative insight and cultural range unmatched by any of his contemporaries. Moreover, even before reaching his thirties he had acquired experience of significant building, effectively graduating with the remarkable apartment block in Avenue de Versailles, Paris.

Yet while this unique curriculum vitae gave Lubetkin huge advantages over his new English colleagues it also presented him with special difficulties. At the very moment he was ready to develop his distinctive architectural vision he was constrained by the fledgling state of British modernism and by larger problems of transition and timing in the movement generally which had occurred around the period of his arrival.

Reyner Banham characterised this reductive change in modernism from the 1920s to the 1930s as a 'decision to fight on a narrowed front'. He wrote –

with the International Style outlawed politically in Germany and Russia, and crippled economically in France, the style and its friends were fighting for a toehold in politically-suspicious Fascist Italy, aesthetically indifferent England and depression-stunned America. Under these circumstances it was better to advocate or defend the new architecture on logical and economic grounds than on grounds of aesthetics or symbolisms that might stir nothing but hostility.[3]

Experiencing the 'culture shock' of English social convention after the ideological turmoils of Russia and Europe, and now embarking in a foreign environment where new commissions would be a function of pure serendipity, Lubetkin found himself obliged to promote his professional credentials in terms of the economic and functional advantages of modern architecture as a deliberate and disingenuous marketing strategy. Tecton's house style would only compound this problem of misrepresentation in the way their didactic justification of design solutions – embracing everything from site logistics to ironmongery details – underscored the apparent primacy of functional considerations in every aspect of architectural decision making.

In consequence, at least in the initial context of public relations, Lubetkin's deeply ingrained formal and artistic preoccupations were largely suppressed, or rather, 'privatised'. The Tecton benchmark became a standard from which to measure deviation, such that Lubetkin himself would soon be judged through the non-compliance of his work with his own marketing. His increasingly embattled position might be characterised as that of one fighting on two fronts – against the traditional architectural establishment obviously, with its outdated values and techniques, but also against his own contemporaries for – as he once put it to me – 'their shamefaced attitude to any kind of artistic will'.

By the mid-1930s he was berating not only the obstructive effect of outmoded building regulations and conservative district surveyors, but also the lack of critical self-appraisal within the modernist camp itself. 'The result', he wrote, 'is that at present it is almost impossible to judge objectively the aesthetic qualities of a building … and we see a return to the functionalist doctrine. If modern architecture is to make the progress of which it is capable, it should go without saying that every building fulfills the purpose for which it is intended; this should be the starting point, not the ultimate criterion.'[4]

The description of his own house in Whipsnade in 1936 reveals the frustration of a poet whose audience is only ready to hear prose:

It is not a 'Modern House' a 'shelter' which, according to professors, should be self-obliterating, unselfconscious and insignificant in its hygenic anonymity; a thing of which one can only say that it is made of reinforced concrete … It does not try to prove that its design grew naturally from the

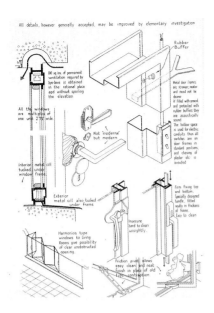

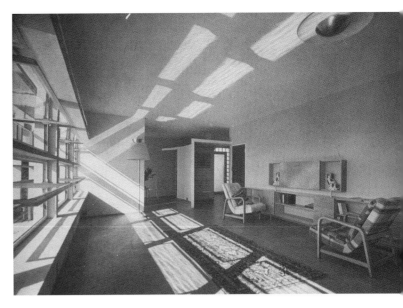

given conditions like an ordinary pumpkin or deep-sea fish. On the contrary the designer admits that there is on the walls of the WC a collection of cold-blooded tropical butterflies, while the bedspreads have little bells sewn on to them to brighten the dreams of the occupants.[5]

To gauge the anomalous nature of this declamation, and of other similar Lubetkinisms around this time, it is necessary to remember the local context. This was when the Modern Architectural Research (MARS) Group was just beginning to find its voice – having disbarred people like Howard Robertson whose main crime (prior to designing the Shell Centre) was to write a book called *Architectural Composition* – when Wells Coates, F.R.S. Yorke, Connell, Ward and Lucas were still setting out modern architecture's spartan stall. It was not the time for irony or humour – modern architecture was battling for its very survival. Indeed, if you will forgive the somewhat contrived link, there was serious *iconoclasm* to get on with – dismantling the establishment hegemony – and the new cause of modernism was too radical and important to be swept under the *carpet*.

So what were the creative sources that Lubetkin had brought with him from his exotic roots, that were so alien to the English cultural environment and his new professional circle? Two of his most important formative influences – icons and carpets – make as good a starting point as any. Lubetkin recalled vividly the impact of that quintessentially Russian artistic tradition – the icon – from the great Exhibition of Ancient Painting in Moscow in 1913 when he was hardly more than a precocious schoolboy.

All of a sudden the sheer splendour of this art burst on us like a revelation, summing up the entire course of Russian art. Some were 13th century icons from Novgorod, some were 15th century produced by the monks of Novodevichi Monastery. Others were Baroque ones of the 17th century Moscow School of Stroganov. But others had been made only yesterday by the village signwriter or some itinerant craftsman, and they combined centuries old traditions with authentic inventiveness and originality, saying what no one had dared to say before.[6]

Apart from its nostalgia, indeed perhaps even chauvinism, two points surely stand out from this sort of evidence. First Lubetkin's propensity for time-travel – his ease in connecting artifacts over a span of 600 years right up to the day before – suggesting the error in seeing artists of his calibre as drawing a line

Figure 3. Window exegesis. Typical example of the explanatory graphics employed by Tecton to market a functional interpretation of modern architecture, 1935.

Figure 4. Lubetkin's bungalow at Whipsnade, 1936 – 'Brightening the dreams of the occupants ... not a Modern House'. (Dell & Wainwright)

5. B. Lubetkin, 'Bungalows at Whipsnade', *Architectural Review*, vol.81, 1937, p.60.

6. B. Lubetkin, 'The Origins of Constructivism', 1969. Quoted in J. Allan, *Berthold Lubetkin – Architecture and the Tradition of Progress*, London, RIBA Publications, 1992, p.24.

across history and separating modernism from previous cultures. Wells Coates once remarked 'we must remember that the past is not always behind us, but more often in front – blocking the way'. Lubetkin on the other hand seems from the very outset to have understood modernism's task as not to reject the past, but to find a valid and creative relationship to it.

The second is surely his perception of the icon as primarily a social statement (even when couched in sacred phraseology) such that it was always narrative, often polemical and potentially even subversive. Thus from Lubetkin's perspective the traditional holy icon could be read as a specialised genre of religious propaganda – in effect a sort of refined billboard to canvas devotion from a suggestible and illiterate audience.

Lubetkin always referred to art as 'a weapon'. 'All art is a kind of propaganda,' he used to say, 'but it has to be art to be any good'. By this he meant the special capacity of art (so pivotal in his Russian experience) to incite the emotions of its audience and thereby operate as an agent of change. His formative years had revealed the link between the icons (and that indigenous sub-genre, the *lubki*) and the agitational art of the early revolutionary period with which Lubetkin identified himself so strongly. Both functioned as a medium of mass communication. Both traditions exploited the flat surface, the stylised image or 'visual slogan', the aggregation of components – whether the traditional iconostasis or the massed placards – to produce cumulative installations of declamatory power. And just as the icons spoke to a pre-revolutionary audience, so the agit trains and ships spoke to a revolutionary one, with a further expansion of the same tradition into the streets and squares in the fabrication of make-believe buildings which the Constructivists could only dream of.

So how does this relate to Lubetkin's personal development and specifically the artistic sensibilities he brought to England in the 1930s? I would contend that because of the impressionable age at which the huge drama of the Revolution was played out before him, these two-dimensional traditions of visual rhetoric with all their energy and urgency were, so to speak, *absorbed*

Figure 5. Iconostasis at Novodevichy Convent, late 17th century, by Klim Mikhailov, from Boris Brodsky, *Art Treasures from the Moscow Museums,* Moscow, Izobrazitelnoye Iskusstvo Publishers, 1980.

Figure 6. The icon as propaganda. Victor Deni's parody of the White Russian leadership in the Civil War, c.1920, from David Elliott, *New Worlds,* London, Thames & Hudson, 1986.

Figure 7. Cardboard Constructivism, c.1921. Typical polemical 'building' installation of the early post-revolutionary period – here used to promote steel production in the Don Basin, from David Elliott, *New Worlds,* London, Thames & Hudson, 1986.

rather than learnt. They were so intrinsic to the formation of his artistic vision that they pre-dated his conscious self-education as an architect. Or, to use current parlance, they were a signalling system hard-wired into his creative toolbox, long before he had even become a professional. Examples survive from even his earliest student days.

Translated into architectural terms, it suggests that the communicative role of two-dimensional elevational design, articulated surfaces, the 'talking façade', or, to use that most taboo of terms in the context of the 1930s, *composition*, was to Lubetkin so instinctual, so innate, as to have none of the reactionary associations that concerned orthodox modernists – preoccupied as they were with the de-materialisation of the wall-as-canvas in favour of the wall-as-plane, as a spatial agent in the formation of solids and voids.

This is directly related to a no less significant point of difference – Lubetkin's experience of classicism as an architectural inheritance. For most modernists their classical training in Beaux-Arts conventions, façade design and specifically the Orders was a yoke to be cast off. 'I knew it like a game played out ... and turned in a gesture of moral revulsion from everything I had been taught', later recalled the English modernist Maxwell Fry of his orthodox professional education at the Liverpool School.[7] For Lubetkin, however, seeing beyond its literal vocabulary, classicism with its traditions of clarity and precision, and modernism with its social and programmatic agenda could share the same intellectual environment. If Lubetkin had an argument with traditional elevations, it was not that they talked, but what they said.

Unlike his disaffected contemporaries, Lubetkin had experienced his training and his 'rebellion' in the opposite order – his engagement with the Russian post-revolutionary upheavals preceding and thus 'conditioning' his professional education. Lubetkin's classicism had been absorbed through his reading of architectural history, on his avid European travels and most significantly through his voluntary attachment to the French master Auguste Perret at the Ecole des Beaux Arts in the mid-1920s. With his disdain of diplomas and his

7. Maxwell Fry, *Autobiographical Sketches*, London, Elek Books Ltd, 1975, p.136.

95

selective approach to class attendance, Lubetkin had no equivalent of Maxwell Fry's Pauline conversion from traditional rote learning to a modern sensibility. Lubetkin had learned what he wanted to learn. He seems instinctively to have been able to reach beyond classicism's recondite stylistic constraints, that to Fry and his peers seemed so tired and irrelevant, and perceive the core values beyond – the preoccupation with human scale, the legibility of organisation, the order and pervasive sense of ceremony.

So how did these profound formative differences affect Lubetkin in the English milieu and the reception of his work by the local audience? If one takes what is commonly regarded as his premier work, Highpoint I, it is immediately

Figure 8. The wall as container – Highpoint II's cubic envelope conceals its internal columns and beams to serve as a metaphor for an ideal structure, yet its final composition is every bit as deliberate and fastidious as that of its neighbour, Highland II. (Dell & Wainwright).

clear how this spartan monolith, with its planar volumetric character, was so easily adopted by the local Modern Movement and how its sequel, Highpoint II, with its articulate surface expression, its luxuriant contrast of man-made and natural geometry, its sophisticated entrance, was so controversial. To the local audience this suggested a return to 'decoration' – or at least evidence of a suspiciously deliberate exercise in composition. To Lubetkin it was a contemporary interpretation of classical syntax, an attempt to speak in articulate language. While both blocks were a clear expression of their respective structure, a Functionalist's wishful belief that Highpoint I's façade was 'nothing but' its structure (ignoring Lubetkin's fastidious control of form, proportion, line and fenestration, not to mention the contorted structural manipulations of Ove Arup needed to achieve it[8]) suggested modern architects were now liberated from the traditional problems of composition.

And so the critique of Highpoint II in *Focus II* (1938) by Anthony Cox,[9] to which reference has been made in every subsequent review of this building, indicted Lubetkin on the most serious charge for which a modernist in England could be accused – a preoccupation with 'ideas as a motive force in design', or to use the 'F' word itself – Formalism – as if this single term were sufficient either as analysis or censure. Seldom can a critique have so perfectly matched the mood of its intended audience – the generation-in-waiting impatient to supersede Lubetkin's achievement.

As Cox was later to elaborate, 'We were not interested in architecture as a cultural object for the individual, nor as a status symbol for the official or

8. Ove Arup, 'Arup Associations', *Architectural Review*, vol. 993, November 1979, pp.315–317

9. A. Cox, 'Highpoint Two, North Hill, Highgate', *Focus II*, 1938, pp.76–9.

commercial organization. The notion of the monument in architecture was anathema, and so was what we called the 'prima donna' architect. Equally suspect was the crystallization of architecture into a particular formal style.'[10]

Although both Highpoints were included in the first statutory roll-call of outstanding Modern Movement buildings, the so-called 'Pevsner list' of 1970, it took Highpoint II more than 30 years to catch up with the grade of its older cousin when both were eventually raised to Grade I. But in the minds of many observers, especially those of the generation of Anthony Cox and immediately following, Highpoint II would never be regarded on equal terms with its neighbour.

The scar left by its perceived betrayal, by its 'divergence' from 'the cause', never healed. Yet looked at now, without the mindset of a Functionalist zealot, it is abundantly obvious that each building is of comparable significance in driving forward the architectural progression of the 1930s, and that they need each other to relate the development of English modernism and of Lubetkin himself, neither of which could possibly have been 'frozen' in 1935 at Highpoint I's completion – however exhilarating and glamorous that moment might have seemed at the time. Indeed, considered in the extended perspective of the post-war period the constructional and architectural themes explored in Highpoint II, with its (then) exploratory eclectic material expression and prototypical frame and cross-wall structure, could be seen to have had by far the greater historical reach.

What I am trying to do is to detach the conventional, Anglo-centric, historiographic template from the interpretation of Lubetkin's work and discover an alternative way of understanding it as a product of his exotic provenance and his oblique relationship to the Modernist cause. So let's talk about the exotic – which the dictionary reminds us simply means foreign, 'originating in a foreign country, not native, having a strange or bizarre allure, beauty or quality 16th century from Latin *exoticus*, from the Greek *exotikos* foreign, from *exo*, outside. Which reminds me how Lubetkin always preferred to describe himself as an outsider, a rootless journeyman. Which in its turn recalls George Steiner's observation that 'the Jew has his anchorage not in place but in time, in his highly developed sense of history as personal context'.[11]

Figure 9. The wall as canvas – Highpoint II's talking façade expresses its structure and becomes a composition of articulate surfaces. Caryatids stand as a human signal, and suggest the canopy is supported with ease. (Lubetkin also intended, in Prokofiev's phrase, that they should 'enrage the stupid'.) (Dell & Wainwright)

Figure 10. Detail of the Gorilla House, London Zoo, 1933, with its Corinthian capital suggesting a symbolic link across time. (Herbert Felton)

10. 'Architects' Approach to Architecture', RIBA Journal, Third series, vol. 174, June 1967, p. 232.

11. G. Steiner, 'A Kind of Survivor', *A Reader*, London, Penguin, 1984.

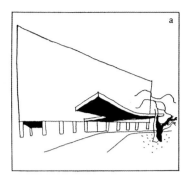

So, resuming our inspection of Highpoint II, we confront the caryatids – another glimpse of Lubetkin the traveller. As Furneaux Jordan remarked, 'to dine out at Highpoint I, and arrive past the caryatids of Highpoint II just when the dark foliage is catching the lights, is to be so ineffably abroad'.[12] Yet these should not have been such a surprise if observers had been paid sufficient attention to the clues Lubetkin had left from the very beginning. I refer to that Corinthian capital which can be seen placed as a sort of classical talisman in early photos of the Gorilla House – surely an embryonic caryatid. It is clear however that a measure of irony has been added in Lubetkin's mock-functionalist justification for the use of these figures through a typically Tectonic comparative analysis of less suitable alternatives.

Building on those Whipsnade disclaimers, this deliberate parody of modernism's own methodology apparently infuriated contemporaries even more than the caryatids themselves, but it is the figures' affirmation that architecture has a storyline beyond the mere demonstration of its own technical solutions that differentiates Lubetkin's mission from that of his contemporaries and suggests we are entering the world of metaphor.[13] For unlike the nearest prior example, the 'brand new' caryatids at St Pancras Church, the Highpoint casts are of *damaged* Acropolis figures, thus serving as symbols of time past and signifying the relativity of modernism's preoccupation with a supposedly unending present.

Upstairs, as if to reinforce the point beyond any possible doubt, the penthouse on the rooftop of Highpoint II was certainly the most personal statement of Lubetkin's artistic vision as anything in his entire oeuvre. And it surely bears out the continuing vitality of those early Russian experiences. The cosy 'datcha-like' space around the fireplace, the animal pelts turned to functional use as in the cabin of a resourceful trapper, the Pollock theatre prints 'flyposted' like peasant *lubki* on the kitchen wall, the rough timber boarding recalling Russia's ancient traditions of wooden construction, the prominence given to his own favourite 'icon' – an old *trompe l'oeil* Dutch tryptich, which he used to explain not as a decorative accessory but rather as a visually coded inventory of the social priorities of its period. The Calder mobiles, the Pajot marines, the enlarged amoeba door lining, the Leger gouache – acquired directly from the painter himself.

Alan Powers has referred elsewhere to the penthouse's 'overt decorative Surrealism'[14] with what I detect as a hint of disparagement. This may or may not provide a stylistic classification, but I prefer to associate Lubetkin's vision with Colin Rowe's thesis of another interpretation of modernity, in contradis-

Figure 11. Lubetkin's alternative options appraisal – a: too light, b: too heavy, c: too thin, d: too personal – an ironical functionalist justification for using caryatids. (Berthold Lubetkin)

Figure 12. The Penthouse, Highpoint II, 1938 – Lubetkin's personal vision of an 'other' modernity embracing memory, time and allusion. (John Havinden)

tinction to the supposed mainline of Gropius, Meyer, and Marinetti: a counter-formulation represented by such artists as Stravinsky, Joyce, Picasso, Eliot and Proust that embraces metaphor, irony and multiple meaning.[15] A tradition that accommodates humanity *and* its past. This difference could hardly be better illuminated than by recalling how Lubetkin placed himself vis-a-vis Marinetti.

> *He was speaking about speed, engines, battleships, the benefits of tourism, of fist fights and smashed furniture, while we were drinking tea around the samovar, thinking of honey and dusty roads, of accordions floating high over the telegraph wires above the silver birches and the meadows.* [16]

What I am trying to suggest is that underneath Lubetkin's radical intellectual and professional stance lay an exotic inner landscape filled with images of Chagall, Pushkin, old Russia and its perishable folklore, and that both in the 1930s (and since) the inspirational influence on his artistic personality of this rare and largely inaccessible inheritance has been consistently neglected or reduced by British observers in the effort to accommodate him within our local category system. As David Sylvester once wrote, 'allegiance to one's own civilisation is largely an allegiance to its iconography: once iconography is irrelevant, all civilisations are equal.'[17]

As well as icons I also mentioned carpets, and without reference to this other formative and vital creative resource it would be impossible to understand the progression of Lubetkin's work from the 1930s towards its social fulfilment in his major post-war housing projects.

> *As far as I remember,* he once wrote of his first intimations of an artistic vocation, *it all started in the dim past when, spellbound, I watched a grown-up finger meandering among lion-headed serpents in the rainless gardens of a wall-carpet.*[18]

This ancient craft of carpet making, which he encountered through his early years in Russia, then studied formally at the Berlin Textile Academy and later on a special scholarship in Vienna, was also understood by Lubetkin as a tradition of two-dimensional visual communication – the stylised motifs and formal conventions containing densely coded information of the makers' history, myths and location. And carpets continued to crop up in his travels, next at the Paris Exhibition of 1925, where he assisted in the realisation of the Melnikov pavilion and related kiosks, some of which served as carpet stalls.

Figure 13. A statement of social priorities. Lubetkin's 17th-century Dutch *trompe l'oeil* tryptich, actually painted on a flat board. (Berthold Lubetkin)

Figure 14. Example of a typical garden carpet employing formalized motifs to represent plots, pathways, planting, streams and fish. *(from 'Islamic Carpets', Arts Council, Exhibition Catalogue, 1972)*

> *It was an important formative period as it taught me to link the purely geometrical compositions, whether plans, whether carpets, with an outlook on the world in philosophical terms. All composition involves a deliberate choice of relation of parts, an internal organisation reflecting in outline the concept of order we believe in.*[19]

Such unashamed use of the term 'composition' might seem unexceptionable now, yet as soon as reconstruction began after the war Lubetkin resumed his criticism of the movement his earlier work had done so much to foster. Already, in explaining his intentions in Spa Green, Tecton's first post-war housing project, he was complaining that,

> *For too long modern architectural solutions were regarded in terms of abstract principles with formal expression left to itself as a functional resultant. The principles of composition, the emotional impact of the visual, were brushed aside as irrelevant. Yet this is the very material with which the architect operates; it is in this sphere that he is sole master, by virtue of his training and tradition ... Turning utility, practicality and functional economy of resources into the sole criterion of quality is the best way to divest architecture of that living richness and complexity that have throughout history given it significance and purpose.*[20]

If the post-war British national housing drive is generally characterised by its concentration on social, technical and economic considerations – all of which

12. R. Furneaux Jordan, 'Lubetkin', *Architectural Review*, vol. 113, July 1955, pp.36–54.

13. See Allan, *op cit.* p.297. Anthony Chitty, a Tecton partner, later wrote, 'The caryatid pillars at Highpoint II were a piece of whimsy we could all accept, but some of us thought Lubetkin's attempt to defend their inclusion as functional quite ridiculous'. Letter to the author, 13 December 1971.

14. A. Powers, 'The Search for a New Reality', *Modern Britain 1929–1939*, London Design Museum 1999, p.37

15. C. Rowe, & F. Koetter, *Collage City*, Cambridge MIT Press 1978, pp.137–43.

16. B. Lubetkin, 'The Origins of Constructivism', *op.cit.*

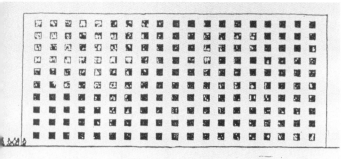

Figure 15. Humanising the slab. Tecton sketch showing (left) the raw ingredients of an elevation, and (right) how compositional intervention gives it scale, rhythm and architectural order. (Berthold Lubetkin)

Figure 16. The cross wall (boxframe) structure of Spa Green (1943–50) – an open canvas for expressive infill. (Sydney Newbery)

Figure 17. Example of paired or jufti knot used in Oriental and Caucasian carpets, studied by Lubetkin in Russia and at the Berlin Textile Academy, 1922–3. (*Islamic Carpets*, Arts Council Exhibition Catalogue, 1972)

17. D. Sylvester, 'On Western attitudes to Eastern carpets', Essay in *Islamic Carpets from the Collection of Joseph V. McMullan*, London, Arts Council of Great Britain, 1972.

18. B. Lubetkin, *Samizdat by Anarchitect*, Unpublished personal memoir, 1978. Quoted from J. Allan, *op.cit.* p.21.

19. B. Lubetkin, 'A Commentary on Western Architecture', O.U. History of Architecture and Design, A305/27. 1975.

20. B. Lubetkin, 'Flats in Rosebery Avenue, Finsbury.' *Architectural Review*, vol. 109, 1951, pp.138–40.

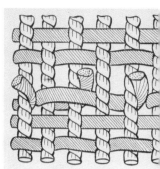

equally of course conditioned the development of Tecton's work – the distinctive aspect of Lubetkin's contribution is his refusal to regard the reconstruction challenge 'simply' as a delivery problem, and his concern to give equal attention to issues of aesthetics, composition and expression.

In architectural terms the situation might be crudely defined as the point in modernism's development at which the problems of surface and scale were added to the more familiar themes of mass and volume. Lubetkin's evolving treatment of these can be traced through his own housing projects. Discounting the special circumstances of their ground and top floors, 25 Avenue de Versailles and Highpoint I were both only six flats high, and one flat wide. Their architectural expression was a limited and direct function of their volumetric organisation. Highpoint II (again discounting the exceptions at ground and roof level) was also six flats high though four flats wide, but here the central portion comprising duplex units formed in framed structure and differently planned were logically differentiated from the outer pair, thus allowing an overall compositional variety.

But what of the new post-war apartment blocks which might be up to ten flats high and eight flats wide, comprising 80 identical units? A single elevation might entail the organisation (that is *composition*) of up to 200 windows. To Lubetkin, this was not just a problem of domestic design – it was an act of urban declamation. In the terms of his early Russian experiences such an elevational task might be equated to designing a 16,000 sq. ft. billboard to last for 80 years.

In the light of what has been said already, it is surely not surprising that faced with compositional challenges of this magnitude Lubetkin should have reached deep into his artistic vocabulary and perceived the linkage between the repetitive nature of the contemporary façade and the rhythmic patterns of traditional carpet making, the ancient craft he had studied in his early travels. In his allusive and philosophical mind the cross-wall structure and floor plate strata of the blocks' construction were a precise equivalent of the warp and weft of the traditional carpet.

The large housing blocks resulting from those economic conditions isolated and underlined the special problem of the elevation, but we could not accept a method that treated it as merely the diagrammatic projection of the plan. An elevation expresses something, it pleads for it. Those blocks must face the street and the people. They could be like a pyramid, enigmatic and inscrutable, or they could try to tell them stories about the world by affirming one of its fundamental laws – that it develops through the interplay of internal contradictions that generate change through the continuous process of becoming.[21]

It is also hardly surprising that in the austere atmosphere of the time the sophistication of Lubetkin's approach found little favour or even comprehension in the contemporary critical audience. Such overt concern for visual enrichment surely offended the hard-won empirical canon of modern architecture – regardless of whether any functional requirements were actually being compromised in the process.

'Façade treatments do not form part of the common theory of the Modern Movement as our elders and betters have it', declared Reyner Banham in 1954. 'In the pure theory the problem of the façade does not exist; form follows function, and when the problems of the interior have been correctly resolved, the exterior form will be found to have crystallized into an unarguable solution.'[22]

Yet the continuing care and conscientiousness of Lubetkin's work in this respect, and indeed its surviving popularity, make a compelling alternative case, and in view of the subsequent castigation of orthodox modernism for its relentless poverty of expression it is surely a case that could now be seen to be vindicated.

John Summerson famously defined the distinctive contribution of modern architecture as *social*, and suggested that its source of unity was to be found in the architect's programme. 'The programme', he argued, 'was the description of spatial dimensions, spatial relationships and other physical conditions required for the convenient performance of specific functions … and the resultant unity … is the unity of a process.'[23] Fifty years ago, when this

21. Lubetkin in conversation with the author, September 1979.

22. R. Banham, 'Façade', *Architectural Review*, vol.116, 1954, p.303.

23. J. Summerson, 'The Case for a Theory of "Modern" Architecture', RIBA *Journal*, vol. 64, June 1957, pp. 307–13.

Figure 18. Caucasian classic dragon rug, (compare with 14). *[from* Islamic Carpets, *Arts Council, Exhibition Catalogue 1972*

Figure 19. Façade detail of Sivil House, Bethnal Green, London, by Skinner, Bailey & Lubetkin, 1964. (John Allan)

pronouncement was made, it might have seemed sufficient. Yet the self-absorption in its own operational brief that such a definition suggests, with its inhibited silence on the emotional content of buildings and implicit justification for designing only 'from the inside out', could now be recognised as a fateful corollary of modern architecture's persistent failure to present a smiling public face. Likewise, looking back, it is easier to see how the modernists' commonplace citation of D'Arcy Thompson in support of the concept of organic architectural form failed to acknowledge the extent to which Nature's outcomes are also a response to *external* environmental factors.

Lubetkin's contribution, by contrast, contradicts modernism's disingenuous denial of the role of personal judgement in design, and deliberately attempts to exploit architecture's traditional capacity to communicate messages and metaphors beyond the mere demonstration of its own constructional logistics. This distinction between the operational obligations of building and the 'fictive body' of architecture is well summarized in Arthur Drexler's essay 'Engineers' architecture, truth and its consequences' which appropriately introduced the most substantial recent survey of the architecture of the Ecole des Beaux Arts – that same tradition which Lubetkin's contemporaries had generally considered was of no relevance to the modern architectural project.

> *Until the advent of the utilitarian engineering style, architecture always and everywhere insisted upon the distinction between itself and building. The former is the domain of freedom of action, conscious choice, and ulterior motives; the latter is the domain of minimum effort in response to external necessity ... Architecture entails a conscious effort to establish a hierarchy of values ...What we may now see as the common ground of all historic styles is not structure, as radical thought in the 19th and 20th centuries concluded, but rather the built metaphorical image by which value is declared.*[24]

Study of Lubetkin's oeuvre in the awareness of his formative sources reveals that in addition to his well-noted social and political concerns, his *architectural* project attempted a reinterpretation of that communicative tradition in a contemporary idiom. He belongs in the select company of artists and composers of the modern era who understood modernism's dependence on its heritage, and who instead of suppressing the past sought to 'metabolise' it.

I have concentrated on icons and carpets because I wanted to get beyond the familiar and unhelpful caricatures of Lubetkin's 'formalism' and explore

Figure 20. Étoile, Paris, with Arc de Triomphe carrying the 'spatial vector' from Place de la Concorde. *(photo: Lecomte, Editions Guy)*

Figure 21. Spatial vectors at Peterlee New Town, 1950. Diagrammatic representation of Lubetkin's unrealised concept of the town centre as a triaxial spatial vortex, anchored by three urban markers. (Drawing: John Allan)

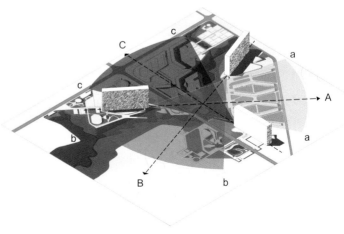

Figure 22. *Trompe l'oeil* aedicule to main axis at Cranbrook Estate, Tower Hamlets, London by Skinner, Bailey & Lubetkin, 1965. (John Allan)

Figure 23. *Prospettiva* by Francesco Borromini, Palazzo Spada, Rome, a 17th-century source of inspiration for Lubetkin's Cranbrook *trompe l'oeil*.

the fertile ground of his artistic memory. A similar quest would discover the ways in which other early sources of inspiration influenced the planning work of his later career and informed his distinctive vision of urban space.

This survey would link such vital formative experiences as his youthful contemplation of the Neva from Vassilievsky Island in St Petersburg, or Arc de Triomphe from Place de la Concorde in Paris, with the concept of the 'spatial vector' – the notion of urban space energised, and thereby made legible, by its architectural coordinates. Though usually submerged in the story of Peterlee as a political and bureaucratic fiasco it is this strategy that underlay the extraordinary unfulfilled design of its town centre and was variously realised in his final housing projects[25] – culminating in that *trompe l'oeil* monument at Cranbrook, a sort of farewell tribute to his inspirational mentors, in this instance Francesco Borromini. The difficulty of communicating such historically laden propositions in the mundane context of welfare state Britain in no way diminishes the integrity of their underlying intention. Indeed, in a paradoxical way, their appreciation may even become easier with the passage of time as they acquire their own historical patina. As Lubetkin himself wrote in 1955,

> *Both baroque and classicism were in fact laboratories where the artificial atmosphere of the historic heights was maintained; the masquerade in both cases was necessary in order to lift sordid reality on to a pedestal. In both cases behind the masquerade lie grandiose spatial conceptions; on the one hand of monistic cohesion and on the other of cool analytical differentiation – penetrating intelligence combined with splendid vision: and in the synthesis of both lies the hope of modern architecture.*[26]

In conclusion – on the one hand Berthold Lubetkin is widely regarded as the most accomplished architect of his generation to have practised in England, being cited by some commentators as one of very few in his professional cohort to achieve 'world standing' on account of his key works, most of which have been listed.

On the other hand his critical positioning has always been problematic, his career trajectory usually being described as a steeply rising gradient that peaked early and thereafter declined in a long downward curve. Specifically, his considerable post-war housing achievement, comprising a far greater out-

24. A. Drexler, 'Engineer's Architecture, Truth and its Consequences', *Architecture of the Ecole des Beaux Arts*, London, Secker & Warburg, 1977, pp.13–59.

25. J. Allan, 'Lubetkin and Peterlee', in Thomas Deckker, ed., *The Modern City Revisited*, London, Spon Press, 2000, pp.103–124.

26. B. Lubetkin, unpublished notebooks, *c.*1955. Quoted from *Allan, J. op cit.* p.534.

put than that of the 1930s, has long been undervalued. Then, bizarrely, in 1982 with the award of the Royal Gold Medal, he was reclaimed as a hero of the Modern Movement and ended his life as an honoured veteran. There is an ironic symmetry in Lubetkin being dubbed a formalist in an age of austerity and a functionalist in an age of affluence. It is the reflex of a culture disinclined to admit the interdependence of art and science, of emotion and reason. Yet as Lubetkin himself used to say, 'utility is the pursuit of purpose, but all purposes are born of emotion. Thus a purpose without emotion would produce utility without purpose.'

From our present historical vantage point, however, it is possible to consider an alternative interpretation, which supersedes his distracting non-compliance with the orthodox modernist template and encompasses the whole span of his oeuvre for what it attempted. Such a rediscovery might then acknowledge that the same exotic sensibilities and historical sophistication that occasioned such criticism from his audience in their day – and which through their consistent neglect by more conventional modernists duly provoked such catastrophic alienation of their audience later – have actually turned out to be the crucial factor that makes his contribution so rich and so durable.

Put another way, while the pretext and focus of the conference at which this paper was originally given were prompted by the exhibition 'Modern Britain 1929–39', to understand Lubetkin you have to look outside the temporal and geographical boundaries suggested by this title. Berthold Lubetkin was a part and a product of the Modern Movement unquestionably, but he was also one of its earliest and most intelligent critics. His vision extended far beyond its immediate programme and his work constantly challenged its self-imposed limitations. Only by studying outside his period can one begin to appreciate his contribution within it. Or, to return to my opening references, despite that fortuitous coincidence of dates, on no account place Lubetkin in the narrow context of 'The International Style'. And never be persuaded that 'complexity and contradiction' were discovered in 1966, or that the work of an architect of Lubetkin's calibre did not always embody such values.

7 KENSAL HOUSE: THE HOUSING CONSULTANT AND THE HOUSED

ELIZABETH DARLING

KENSAL HOUSE: THE HOUSING CONSULTANT AND THE HOUSED

ELIZABETH DARLING

Anyone who is already familiar with the architecture of the 1930s, or who opens a book to find out more, will inevitably come across the subject of this paper, Kensal House in North Kensington. Its place within the canon of British modernism is assured, yet how much do we actually know about it? Despite its familiarity, I would suggest very little. What do we know of what the estate was supposed to achieve? If it succeeded in its aims? And, perhaps of particular relevance to this paper, what reality lay behind that long list of people whose names are attached to the project: 'designed by Maxwell Fry (executant architect), who worked in consultation with Robert Atkinson, C.H. James, Michael Tapper, G. Grey Wornum and Elizabeth Denby (Housing Consultant)'[1] I suspect that in common with many people I used to read this list without really thinking what it meant. Then I thought, what *is* a Housing Consultant? Who was Elizabeth Denby? Why should a team of architects design a block of flats? Why should this have featured so prominently in the contemporary coverage of the project?

It is, then, the aim of this paper to try to answer these questions. I shall consider how Kensal House came to be built and who designed it, focusing particularly on Denby. I want then to discuss the estate itself and finally, consider the reception of the estate by its tenants, something it is possible to do because evidence of their views survives.

KENSAL HOUSE

The production of Kensal House should be seen in the context of campaigns by British central governments in the inter-war period to provide affordable housing for the working-class population. In the 1920s, successive governments had focused on the construction of housing estates on virgin sites on the peripheries of existing towns and cities. By the 1930s this policy had changed to one of slum clearance and the construction of blocks of flats on cleared sites in the inner cities.

A second factor behind the decision to build Kensal House was the emergence of the electricity industry as a major competitor to power suppliers like the Gas, Light and Coke Company (GLCC). Municipal building programmes, as well as the concomitant growth of a market in houses built for owner occupation, provided a huge potential market for gas companies. Yet the existence of competition from electricity forced the gas industry to advertise itself, its services and its products as never before in order to retain a share of the market.

The GLCC was at the forefront of the campaign to sell gas. From the late 1920s onwards it sought various means to increase consumption of gas. The company initiated the redesign of its product range and, through a newly founded publicity department, from 1931 promoted fuel consumption through advertisements and film. It also pursued a long-term programme of lobbying government to ensure that gas was used, or made available to be used, in municipal housing schemes. The passing of a series of slum clearance acts in 1930, 1933 and 1935 gave renewed impetus to the company's campaigns to create demand for its products.

Figure 1. Kensal House from Ladbroke Grove (Architectural Press)

1. See *Architects' Journal*, vol.85, 18 March 1937, p.453, for such a list.

The culmination of the drive to promote gas consumption was the decision made in November 1933 to build a block of flats to demonstrate how 'working class tenants could be provided with an all-gas service offering every amenity that a reasonable middle-class family might demand – and this without any abnormal capital outlay and at a running cost within their means'.[2] Initially it seems that the company saw the project entirely as a commercial venture, but almost immediately it was decided that the project might also serve as a means to signify the company's commitment to public service. It was therefore agreed that 'the estate should be an enlightened contribution to rehousing in a wider sense'.[3]

Although the company could provide the necessary technological expertise for the scheme, it had no in-house knowledge of social housing or architecture. So at the same time as the decision to build the flats was taken, the company's director, David Milne Watson, announced the formation of an Architects' Committee 'to advise the Company on architectural and kindred matters of common interest'.[4] Its six members were 'a group of people with unquestionable eminence in the world of housing design' who would work on a number of projects, including the scheme for Kensal House.[5]

Once the team of experts had been assembled, the GLCC chose a site on part of a former gas-works site at Kensal Green, North Kensington. This was in the poorest part of Kensington: the gas-works, in particular, were surrounded by some of the area's worst slums. The scheme would be built on a one and a third acre site and would provide 68 flats. Since this was a scheme to demonstrate how former slum dwellers could be rehoused cheaply and well, it was decided that the company should form a housing association, named the Capitol Housing Association, to build and manage the estate. This semi-public status meant that the GLCC could qualify for state subsidy and would have to adhere to Ministry of Health guidelines.

On the part of its patrons, then, Kensal House was intended to be a model scheme in two main respects: first, of how cheap and socially useful gas power and products could be; and second, to show that private enterprise could, at a time of increasing state intervention, contribute to the nation's well-being and perhaps even improve on what the state could offer. To prove these points, Kensal House would have to be radically different from the state's model of social housing, which, Fry commented, took 'the winding roads and nothing happening' approach to design with their asphalted sites and five-storey balcony access blocks.[6] The company's brief to the Committee was to solve "the problem of providing the right living conditions for re-housed slum dwellers'.[7]

Although the flats are always attributed to the whole Committee, according to the evidence the project was assigned to Denby and Fry only: certainly the right experts to consult if the GLCC wanted an alternative model of social housing. Fry's ardent modernism had led him to a wholehearted engagement with the problem of social housing. He had already developed a prototype block of flats, based on the use of a reinforced-concrete portal truss frame, which he envisaged could go into mass production. A version of this, R.E. Sassoon House, was in preparation when he was appointed to the GLCC 's Architects' Committee.

His collaborator was Elizabeth Denby, who described herself as a 'Housing Consultant'. When Kensal House was opened in March 1937 the publicity stated that she had been recruited for her work 'as a pioneer in connection with certain aspects of housing design and in planning for working-class families'.[8] This does not quite tally with the chronology, for it was precisely at the time of her appointment to the Committee that Denby embarked on her career as a housing consultant. Her membership of the Committee may have come through Fry or equally conceivably because she had already made contact with the GLCC in her previous job as Organising Secretary of the Kensington Hous-

2. Anon, 'Opening of Kensal House', *Co-partners Magazine*, April 1937, p.181.

3. Anon, 'Kensal House', *The Times*, 16 March 1937, p.13.

4. Minutes of the Directors' Court of the Gas, Light and Coke Company, copies held at the London Metropolitan Archive. Meeting held 3 Nov. 1933. B/GLCC /54.

5. 'Opening of Kensal House', p.181.

6. Maxwell Fry, *How Modern Architecture came to England*, audio-visual set, c.1975.

7. 'Opening of Kensal House', p.181.

8. ibid.

ing Association and Trust, which operated in North Kensington where the GLCC was a major employer.

Denby is a fascinating figure, someone who reminds us of the most common way in which women have influenced the form of our built environment, in that she was *not* an architect. She is a little-known figure today, but in the 1930s was widely admired. For example, Astragal in the *Architects' Journal* of September 1936 commented: 'In our little world Miss Denby ... wields more influence – and gets more done – than any six pompous or prating males'.[9] This opinion was ratified when in 1942 she was made an Honorary Associate of the RIBA. The *Architects' Journal* commented:

> in electing Elizabeth Denby to be Honorary Associate, the RIBA has conferred well-deserved recognition on one who occupies a unique position in the architecture world. Her experience in flat management and her researches abroad ... have enabled her to make important contributions to a number of housing schemes. Elizabeth Denby is the star in the profession she invented for herself: 'consultant on low-rental housing'.[10]

What was a housing consultant? Someone who seems to have been entirely of Denby's invention – a figure who would advise on all aspects of the design and management of social housing: its form, its equipment, its furnishing and its programme of social amenities. She was able to do this because she had a broad range of knowledge on all these matters rather than a specialism in one. Denby had invented the role – as far as can be surmised, for she left few personal documents – because she wanted to become involved in the constructional side of slum clearance, something she had not really been able to do in her previous job. She seems to have had a lifelong interest in architecture and design (on occasion designing herself). Having taken a certificate in social science at the London School of Economics in 1917, a training usually intended for social work, Denby first worked at the Ministry of Labour and then in 1923 began a decade's work in the slums of North Kensington. She was employed first by the Kensington Council of Social Service, an umbrella group for voluntary social work in the area, and then by one of its offshoots, the Kensington Housing Association and its building arm, the Kensington Housing Trust, where a contemporary recalled 'her office fizzed with energy, new ideas and alarming outburst ... Elizabeth, always two jumps ahead of everyone else, impossible to catch up with, unpredictable, immensely stimulating'.[11]

It was in North Kensington that Denby learnt the philosophy which would inform her practice in the 1930s: that social work was not just about material improvements to the lives of the poor but spiritual and moral changes too. This reflects the influence of idealist philosophers like T.H. Green and Bernard Bosanquet on the inter-war voluntary sector: the belief that 'the perfection and moral condition of a state is dependent upon the degree of citizenship in its membership'.[12] The only way for society to progress was for all its members to participate fully in its collective life. Thus social welfare should also develop the poor into useful citizens, a matter of urgency in the new mass democracy of the 1930s. Such philosophies and Denby's first-hand knowledge of the living conditions of North Kensington's slum dwellers combined to create what became Denby's theory of housing which she summarised as follows: 'housing wasn't a question of shelter alone, or even firstly, but a question of reclaiming life – of enriching and enlarging the whole sphere of human activities'.[13]

Denby had already begun the process of trying out this philosophy at Sassoon House, a project she had instigated. It is Kensal House, however, which really exemplifies her theory of housing. This is because the choice of what constituted the right living conditions for former slum dwellers seems to have been left entirely to her and Fry, though some hint at what this might entail was given by the company's concern to deal with the social problems associated with housing, particularly 'the best use of leisure time by the mar-

9. Astragal, 'New Homes for Old', *Architects' Journal*, vol.84, 24 September, 1936, p.403.

10. Anon, 'Elizabeth Denby', *Architects' Journal*, vol.95, 11 June 1942, p.400.

11. E. Pepler, 'Elizabeth Denby, Obituary', *Housing Review*, vol.15, January 1966, p.9.

12. A.Vincent & R.Plant, *Philosophy, Politics and Citizenship*, Oxford, 1984, p.2.

13. Elizabeth Denby's speech to Senior Speech day recorded in *Bradford Girls Grammar School Chronicle*, 1944, p.31.

Figure 2. R.E. Sassoon House, Peckham, Elizabeth Denby & Maxwell Fry, 1934 (Architectural Press)

Figure 3. Arial Perspective Drawing of Kensal House (Architectural Press)

Figure 4. Plans of Kensal House flats (Ascot Gas Water Heaters Ltd)

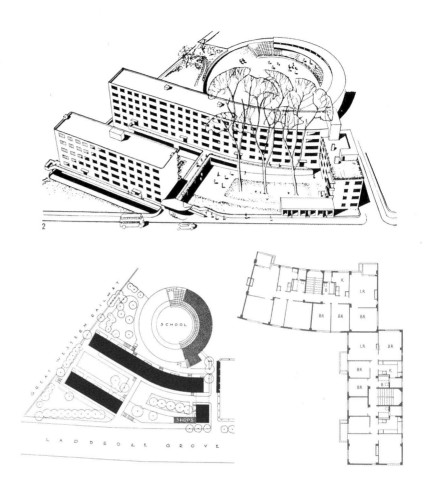

ried folk and young men and women ... the proper care of the bodies and minds of little children too young for school'.[14]

According to Fry, 'Elizabeth and I thought very hard about how the people could live there'.[15] The result, which was finally opened in March 1937, was 'no ordinary block of flats but a community in action, with social rooms, workshop, a corner shop, with larger flats, better balconies, even a separate drying balcony ... and ... a nursery school'.[16] Kensal House would be what Denby called 'an urban village'.[17]

What was meant by a 'community in action'? As Fry's description suggests, it was to be more than just a block of flats. The aim was to create an environment in which the tenants could be transposed from the misery and life-defeating environment of the slums, where family life and decency were perceived as under constant attack, to an estate where family and community life could be restored. This demanded a many pronged solution. Hence in their design of Kensal House, Denby and Fry brought together the services of technology, architecture and social welfare to provide not just for the material needs of the tenants, by building solid, well-planned and well-equipped flats, but also for their social needs through the provision of a range of amenities and facilities. Equal attention was paid to the design of both the private and public parts of the estate and once it was built and inhabited, careful attention was paid to the running and management of the scheme. As far as can be worked out, Denby was responsible for the social facilities and advised on the planning of the kitchens, while Fry provided the architectural setting.

Fry's design was for three, five-storey blocks of flats. The two large blocks ran parallel to the main road, Ladbroke Grove, with their short ends overlook-

14. David Milne Watson (Director of the GLCC) quoted in 'Opening of Kensal House', p.182.

15. Fry, *op.cit.*

16. Maxwell Fry, *Autobiographical Sketches*, London, Elek Books, 1975, p.143.

17. Elizabeth Denby, 'Kensal House, an Urban Village', *The Phoenix*, June 1937, p.12.

ing a railway line; a shorter block stood at right angles to the Grove. The main blocks ran north to south, an early example of the application of *zeilenbau* principles in England, so that living rooms could face west. A reinforced concrete frame was used for each block, with standardised columns and beam units. In between the blocks the space was grassed over and the existing planting retained. Behind the main blocks, the site of a former gas holder was transformed into a children's playground overlooked by the scheme's nursery school.

Each block contained a mix of either two-or three-bedroomed dwellings, accessed by a staircase and with pram and bicycle sheds at ground-floor level. In keeping with the desire to reinvigorate family life, the flats were planned to '[secure] serenity and quietness in the home life of the tenants'.[18] The aim was always to create a strong contrast with the slum homes from which the tenants came. Each flat was, more or less, the same, and contained a large living room (approximately fifteen feet by twelve) and a fully-equipped working kitchen which was a standard unit with the bathroom and lavatory. This was, in effect, an English *existenz-minimum*.

Of the rooms in the flats, the kitchen and living room were seen as the most important by Denby and Fry. The efficient plan and array of equipment in the kitchen served as both a vivid contrast to the cooking facilities available to tenants in their former homes and a location within which the female tenant could develop as a housewife and mother. GLCC publicity stressed that a well-planned kitchen would alleviate the excessive burden of housework which was thought to make the woman 'a worse human being, a worse wife, and a worse mother than she could be'.[19] The kitchen was designed by Denby to be labour-

18. *ibid.*

Figure 5. Kensal House kitchen (Ascot Gas Water Heaters Ltd)

Figure 6. Kensal House living room with furniture from House Furnishing Ltd (AP)

saving, hence its small size (eleven feet by seven feet five inches) which allowed every feature to be within reach. It was extremely well-equipped with a gas copper, spontaneous gas water-heater, continuous work-surfaces, cupboards, and gas iron and cooker. Laundry would be carried out here, and Denby included a drying balcony 'large enough to take sheets and blankets' which led off the kitchen.[20] This meant that washing could be carried out in private and hung up away from prying eyes – a way in which the privacy of the family could be ensured.

The kitchen was thus the wife's workshop where, as Fry explained, 'the important work of the house [could be] carried on without disturbing the life of the living room and with a lighter mind for that blessing'.[21] A door (and a hatch) led from it into the room to which it was a complement, the living room. This was the space where family life would be lived to the full. The smallness of the kitchen meant that the family meals would have to be eaten in the living room, which thereby provided a location for the daily coming together of the family. A coke fire provided the modern equivalent of the family hearth and, since it could not be used for cooking, further reinforced the idea that the living room was not to be a work space. Tenants were able to buy furniture for their new homes from Denby's shop, House Furnishing Ltd, which she had set up in conjunction with the Saint Pancras Housing Improvement Society to bring affordable well-designed furniture (available on hire purchase) to the poor.

From the living room a door led on to a sun balcony which Denby believed to be another vital aspect of the design. It compensated for the lack of a garden, and provided access to fresh air and light. It was designed to be large enough, at eight by five feet, to hold a table or give sufficient space for children to play within sight of their mother. Window boxes were fixed into the balconies which enabled tenants to grow plants or vegetables.

If the individual flats of Kensal House were intended to provide privacy and reinforce family life, the areas outside their front doors were intended to create a location in which the tenants could become a 'community in action'. On leaving their homes, tenants entered the public sphere of Kensal House. Each family belonged to a staircase committee which was responsible for looking after the communal areas around their flats, and from which a representative would be selected to serve on the estate's tenants' committee. On the lower

19. S.C. Leslie, *Kensal House, the Case for Gas is proved*, London, 1937, p.4.

20 Maxwell Fry, 'Kensal House' in Ascot Gas Water Heaters Ltd, *Flats, Municipal & Private Enterprise*, London, 1938, p.58.

21. ibid.

Figure 7. Child on Kensal House balcony
(British Commercial Gas Association)

ground floor of each main block, communal life was also enhanced by the provision of two social clubs which tenants, and others in the surrounding area, could join.

These clubs, one for adults and one for children, were run by an organisation called the Feathers Club Association. This was a voluntary organisation which provided community centres for the poor and unemployed near areas of slum housing. It had been formed in 1935 at the instigation of Denby and was funded by the Prince of Wales and his circle of friends. Feathers Clubs provided not only a space for entertainment, refreshment and meeting, but also workshops with sewing machines and boot-mending equipment so that tenants could make do and mend. The two clubs at Kensal House represented the first time that such an amenity had been built as an integrated part of a new estate and helped to provide a location for the best use of leisure time.

Outside the blocks were further amenities through which communal life would be facilitated. The absence of space and greenery in slum areas was to be replaced by grass and trees and the children's playground. Allotments were

Figure 8. Rear elevation of Kensal House showing sun and drying balconies and the estate's nursery school in the foreground (Ascot Gas Water Heaters Ltd)

laid out for the male tenants, providing them with healthy exercise and cheap food. Overlooking the playground was the estate's nursery school. Mothers from the estate, and those who lived nearby, could leave their children at the nursery all day in the care of a trained nurse. Each child received a daily medical inspection, a dose of cod-liver oil, a healthy meal, plenty of play and fresh air. The focus on childcare is interesting. At this date there was a widespread belief in the voluntary sector that one of the most effective ways to improve the working classes was to start with their children and thereby 'cut the slum tradition off at the root'.

Figure 9. Kensal House's playground (Edith Tudor Hart)

Figure 10. *Children's afternoon nap in the Kensal House nursery school (Ascot Gas Water Heaters Ltd)*

The provision of a nursery and the extensive social programme of the estate were intended to draw out the tenants' potential and give them a sense of their own abilities. A crucial part of this process, and unique for its day, was the establishment of a tenants' committee. This was formed of tenant representatives from the staircase committees and was responsible for the day-to-day running of the estate, with Denby in overall charge as Housing Director.

As far as Denby and Fry were concerned, the combination of particular design features with clearly defined social and welfare provision could transform the lives, and indeed the very natures, of the tenants. The relocation of former slum dwellers into a bright, airy home with amenities at close hand and a tenants' committee to encourage self-responsibility were all means of allowing the poor to reclaim the life denied to them by the slums and become useful citizens. As Denby commented: 'the tenants of Kensal House are to my biased mind a fine example of the latent potentialities in every slum dweller which only need freeing from weed before they flower'.[22]

As produced, Kensal House was intended as a model project in all respects: of what business could do as social service; of what social housing could be in place of the state's approach; and of how to produce that housing through the

22. Elizabeth Denby, 'Kensal House, an Urban Village', in Ascot Gas Water Heaters Ltd, *Flats, Municipal & Private Enterprise*, London, 1938, p.62.

coordinated attack on the problem by a team of experts. That was the idea, but what did the tenants think?

CONSUMING KENSAL HOUSE

For once, we have some idea. A highly mediated example of tenants' views may be gained through the way they were used in advertising of the period, and a less mediated one from the results of a survey taken of the tenants in 1942.

In advertising the tenants were used to get the message across, lending authenticity and a means of identification to potential consumers. The National Smoke Abatement Society's pamphlet 'Britain's Burning Shame' made extensive use of Kensal House to advocate the use of smokeless fuels.[23] Renamed Cleanliness House, it is described as 'an experiment in clean living'. 'Listen to what they say, these are real people and their names are real too!' Mrs Tully was quoted as saying 'my washing doesn't take me half as long'; Mrs Fletcher commented 'I have plenty of time for dress making now' while Mrs Homans drove the point home: 'Give your children clean air at home'.

A similar use is evident in the commercial work of the gas industry itself, Kensal House is featured extensively in its press advertisements. In addition, a film, *Kensal House*, was made by the British Commercial Gas Association in 1937 to promote the scheme and its all-gas provision. Again the emphasis in much of the film is on, ostensibly, letting the tenants speak for themselves. The tenants are full of praise. Mr George Aldridge, the main narrator, contrasts the life of some of the families before and after moving to Kensal House. The Shepherds (a family of nine), for example, are shown living and eating in one room and then in their new flat. Aldridge comments 'plenty of room now for the Shepherd family at dinner time and no cooking in the living room either ... her own kitchen with a gas cooker complete, plenty of cupboards and a hatch to save her legs when the table's being laid'. Similar eulogies are delivered about the nursery and the Feathers Club.

But what was the reaction when the tenants spoke for themselves? In December 1942 the managing director of the GLCC received the results of a survey carried out earlier that year into "what the tenants think of Kensal House".[24] Of the original 68 families, 58 were still in occupation five years later, enough time to have lived with the experiment and gained a perspective on its merits. The research work was done by Marjorie Bruce Milne, a publicity journalist who had worked extensively for the GLCC in the 1930s. She wrote, 'At your express request it is entirely frank.' It is a fascinating document which gives us not just a clear idea of how some of Fry and Denby's ideas did not work in practice, but how ordinary working people viewed their homes at this date.

To be fair, much of the report is positive: 61 of the 68 families believed they were better off at Kensal House and Milne declared 'the water heater at the sink, their own bathroom, the coke grate, the splendid draining boards in the kitchen, the sun balcony and their own wash copper, these the majority would not be without'. In that respect Denby and Fry had responded successfully to working-class needs. There were, however, significant oversights in their designs. Milne noted that three issues came up constantly: dampness, described as 'oozing out of the walls'; noise, in particular from the Feathers Club, exacerbated by the concrete construction and the low ceilings; and the shabby conditions – upkeep does not appear to have been carried out on a regular basis.

Particularly revealing are the tenants' perceptions and use of what Denby and Fry saw as the key rooms in the flats, the living room and the kitchen. Intended as labour-saving and hygienic they were problematic in practice. The drying balcony which Fry declared was large enough to hold sheets and blankets, was not. In reality these had to be folded into four and then got dirty because they flapped against the walls (and this was a site next to the railway). This meant that tenants used the sun balcony instead, although drying laundry

23. National Smoke Abatement Society, *Britain's Burning Shame*, London, c.1938. All quotations are taken from this leaflet.

24. GLCC, 'What the tenants think of Kensal House', unpublished survey carried out by Marjorie Bruce Milne, December 1942. All quotations are taken from this report.

115

there was prohibited, or as in the case of one tenant, dried laundry inside over the cooker with the grill on.

As for the idea that only work should carry on in the kitchen the survey suggests otherwise. Twenty-one families always or sometimes ate in the kitchen 'perched at the ironing board or by the hatch'. One tenant explained, 'we nearly always eat in the kitchen so as to keep the sitting room tidy'. This response was a common one. Tenants did not like the fact that they had only one living space, something which was made particularly problematic by the specific circumstances facing them. Many of the husbands worked outdoors and came home dirty, 'I want somewhere to dry my man's clothes. He does outdoor work. He can't help it but he comes home filthy. Where am I to dry his clothes? There is no room in the kitchen and there is nothing to do with it. It means we have to sit with them here in the evening'.

Another problem was the size of many of the families; most had at least three children, some as many as seven. The kitchen could not cope with such demand and dinner had to be cooked in relays. In addition the wear and tear exacted by large numbers of children on living-room furniture caused heartache for families who had bought new furniture or whose just about respectable settee quickly became shabby. One tenant was recorded as keeping her settee and armchairs in the bedroom and dragged them into the living room only when there were visitors. It was a rather mixed response but, on balance, most tenants agreed that they were much better off at Kensal House than in their previous homes.[25]

CONCLUSION

Kensal House was a project born out of much enthusiasm and optimism: a real desire to produce a project which worked to everyone's advantage. The GLCC would persuade the government of the need for gas and boost its market share and contribute to the well-being of the nation. Denby and Fry would have invented a new type of social housing and thus created more work for themselves, while the tenants would have new homes in which they could develop into healthy and fulfilled citizens.

That it did not quite happen that way was perhaps partly to do with over-ambition on the part of all our protagonists, but was equally the result of bad timing. The outbreak of war just two years after Kensal House opened cannot have helped the running of such an experimental scheme. Secondly, political circumstances, especially after 1945, were not sympathetic to privately funded and locally based social welfare schemes. Nationalisation of the gas industry subsumed the GLCC, who were forced to sell Kensal House to the London County Council (LCC) sometime in the early 1950s. One of the ideas central to Kensal House had been that through the tenants' committee and community facilities like the nursery and the Feathers Club the tenants would feel that they owned and were responsible for their estate. Once the estate belonged to a distant, anonymous landlord like the LCC, opposed to such local practices, Kensal House's days as a community in action were over.

A rather sorry tale; what can I say in conclusion? Alas, Denby's figure of the housing consultant did not survive the war; the forces of professionalisation in architecture and social work combined to close off those worlds to her. But she had achieved much in the 1930s and, today, it seems that many aspects of what she said and did have become familiar to social housing practice. Tenant management and the devolution of ownership is becoming commonplace.

What I hope I have done here is not just increase the body of knowledge about Kensal House but, perhaps more importantly, suggest that what is most interesting about it is not its modernism, but its social programme for which a rather remarkable woman was responsible.

25. For a more detailed analysis of tenants' responses to Kensal House see the author's article 'What the Tenants think of Kensal House: Experts' Assumptions versus Inhabitants' Realities in the Modern Home', *Journal of Architectural Education*, vol.53, March 2000, pp.167–77.

8 THE EDUCATION OF A MODERN ARCHITECT: DENYS LASDUN IN THE 1930S

BARNABAS CALDER

THE EDUCATION OF A MODERN ARCHITECT: DENYS LASDUN IN THE 1930S

BARNABAS CALDER

In 1930, two years after the foundation of the Congrès Internationaux d'Architecture Moderne (CIAM), the year between Wells Coates setting up his office and Berthold Lubetkin coming to London, Denys Lasdun's headmaster's report advised the 16-year-old that 'in considering his future, he should remember to try to utilise his undoubted artistic ability.'[1] Lasdun entered the London architectural world two years later, at a time when modernism was gaining a foothold there. When the Second World War broke out he was still seven days short of his 26th birthday, but already it was clear that he had heeded his headmaster's advice: he had played his small part in the establishment of European modernism in Britain. Most architects would still be in their first job out of school at 25, but Lasdun had already built two houses, come fourth in a national competition, and worked for both Wells Coates and Lubetkin and Tecton. His ascent from drifting schoolboy to accomplished and respected architect was quick and dramatic, and in it lie some roots of the artistic vision which he was to develop to such effect after the war.

At the beginning of the 1930s, Lasdun was at Rugby School. Despite taking pleasure in his art classes he had, according to his elegantly self-deprecating recollections, little ambition beyond a wish not to go to university. Having ended up at the Architectural Association (AA) largely through the initiative of others, he was soon becoming serious about architecture. It appears that he was born with the ability to charm and engage potential clients, as his first commission came in his second year of undergraduate training, completely out of the blue, from a couple he met at a party: 'the couple said they wanted to buy a house and did I know any that were for sale, to which I said, "I think it's ridiculous these days to buy a house, you should build one." After which I got a letter saying, "Well, we'll give you £50 to design our house. We know a site in Oxshott."' Lasdun recalled rising at five in the morning to be able to get back in time for ten o'clock lectures at the AA after supervising work on the site – although 'supervising' may be misleading, as he learnt a great deal about building 'under the instruction of the foreman'.[2]

The resulting house, known as Silver Greys, presumably from the bricks used for its exterior, is rather curious.[3] It is very unlike anything Lasdun would build later, but as the work of a 20-year-old student it is not bad. Unsurprisingly, it exhibits very strong influences from the prevailing thought at the AA of the time and is, as such, a peculiar hybrid. The general effect of the exterior is slightly awkward Arts and Crafts, with pitched roof, brick-mullioned windows and asymmetrical elevations. The other tradition still going strong at the AA was a simplified classicism descended from the highly formal, axially planned schemes of the Ecole des Beaux Arts. At Silver Greys, the curiously formal gesture of a pyramid of steps up to the front door, and the back steps which place the building on a sort of podium, are both reminiscent of these sorts of Beaux-Arts schemes. More explicitly classical is the pair of fluted columns flanking the door. They have no base, no capital and no entasis, and even their visual support for the head of the doorway is equivocal, as they rise

1. William Curtis, *Denys Lasdun: Architecture, City, Landscape*, London, Phaidon, 1994, p.20.

2. Interview with Jill Lever for National Life Story Collection, 1996–7, transcript in the Lasdun archive, pp. 18–19.

3. *Architect and Building News*, vol.142, 28 December 1934, pp.388–9.

Figure 1. 32 Newton Road, 1938. (RIBA Library Photographs Collection).

one course of bricks above it. This kind of modified, stripped-down classical reference can be seen in many British buildings of the period, including, for instance, Grey Wornum's Royal Institute of British Architects (RIBA), London.

To this collision of Arts and Crafts and classicism is added a third influence present in the AA by this time: that of continental modernist theory. This is clearest in the plan, in which can be distinguished various principles being advocated by Le Corbusier and more particularly by Gropius. First, all the living spaces – living room and bedrooms – face south to catch the sun, and their windows are much more generous than those on the north, which only light corridors, bathrooms and other service areas. This kind of clear distinction between served and servant spaces was to remain central to Lasdun's thinking. The 1960s

Figure 2. Silver Greys, 1934, front view.

Figure 3. Silver Greys, rear view.

Figure 4. Silver Greys, plans.

student residences at Christ's College, Cambridge, and those at the University of East Anglia (UEA) both contain entirely windowless access and sanitation, while the rooms themselves are full of light from large south-facing windows.

The second feature of Lasdun's plan which would not look out of place in a modernist house of the period is the opening up of the living room into a single space. There are areas for dining, sitting and work, but no walls interrupting them. A possible borrowing from Le Corbusier is Lasdun's use of the roofs above the garage and the end of the living room as terraces, as advocated in the famous 'five points'. The house is the product of a young architect's selection of recent planning improvements from Europe, contemporary technology in the metal windows, overall appearance from Arts and Crafts, and points of emphasis from the classical tradition. This kind of thoughtful eclecticism is strongly reminiscent of the writings of Howard Robertson, who had just left the AA when Lasdun arrived there.[4] His ethos was clearly still alive in the school. Although Lasdun would never again produce such an undigested blend, he retained this ability to take ideas that he liked from a variety of sources without swallowing the accompanying packages of dogma. He refused at first to join the MARS group (the British representatives at CIAM) when invited by Coates, stating his objection to such attempts to establish orthodoxies, and again after the war he fought against classification as a member of any group, notably rejecting the tag 'Brutalist'.[5]

For his 21st birthday Lasdun received a copy of *Towards a New Architecture*, and was at once excited by its bold and poetically expressed theory. It was not

4. E.G. Howard Robertson, *Modern Architectural Design*, London, Architectural Press, 1932.

5. Letter from Lasdun to Wells Coates, 12 June 1939, Lasdun archive.

long before he profited from a vacation to travel to Paris and look at Le Corbusier's buildings for himself. It was something of a conversion experience for Lasdun, and created in him an admiration for the older architect which was to stay with him throughout his life, and shape his architecture more than any other external source, although he never accepted Le Corbusier's urban theory. The building which affected him most on that visit was the Pavillon Suisse, and the influence is immediately apparent in his third-year project at the AA, for 'An Academy for Colonial and Dominion Scholars in London'. The scheme is by no means a copy of the Parisian model, but the similarity of the disposition of elements and of the architectural language is unmistakable.[6]

As far as Lasdun could recall in later life, it was a summer vacation internship after his third year at the AA which introduced him to Wells Coates's practice. He was attracted there by the obvious Corbusian modernity of the Isokon flats in Lawn Road, at the time recently completed. By the end of the summer, Lasdun had decided that the business of designing and building was much more enjoyable than studying at the AA, and he joined the firm and abandoned his official training.[7] Coates's glamorous association with Le Corbusier and other leading modern architects through CIAM, and his single-minded application of modernist design techniques in both industrial design and architecture, drew promising younger architects to him. In the office at the same time as Lasdun were Patrick Gwynne, who designed the splendid house in Esher for his father while working here, and Edric Neel, who went on to found Arcon and do important work on plastics and prefabrication. The atmosphere was exciting and progressive. Gwynne recalled the group talking about architecture for hours after work, sometimes in the chair-less sitting area in which Coates alone, with his Japanese experience, could achieve comfort while the others squatted awkwardly; and sometimes in the Gargoyle Club, surrounded by Matisse murals, watching Coates sketching on the pristine table-cloths.[8]

During the two years he spent with Coates, Lasdun must have been involved in a number of schemes, but a few seem to have been especially associated with him. The first two were for blocks of flats, one an unbuilt project in Bristol, the other the Palace Gate block in Kensington. Lasdun and Coates worked together on both, elaborating the Russian Constructivist 3:2 section for use in flats for the middle classes.[9] The system involved housing service and sleeping areas beneath an ungenerous eight-foot ceiling, but with living rooms rising to twelve feet for a more elegant space. This permitted three floors of service areas to be accommodated in the same twenty-four-foot rise as two living rooms, allowing simultaneously the economic advantages of density and the pleasure of more luxurious spaces. Lasdun was to revisit the principle in planning his block of flats in St James's Place after the war.

Lasdun recalled in 1995 that his role in the Palace Gate design went further, too: it was his suggestion to pull the main block back from the road and allow the entrance hall to project forwards independently. Previously, as he remembered it, the flats had been going to follow the edge of the site like the firm's Embassy Court in Brighton.[10] By coincidence, Denys Lasdun and his mother lived in a Victorian flat directly opposite the Palace Gate site, giving him a chance to see its innovative constructional techniques close up.

The project on which Lasdun was given most autonomy within Coates's office was their entry to the *News Chronicle* Schools Competition of 1937. This was very substantially the work of Lasdun, and won fourth place, ahead of dozens of schemes, including those by Tecton, and Marcel Breuer and F.R.S. Yorke. The competition required firms to design a school which might feasibly be built without massive expense and which might function without wholesale changes to the curriculum, but it simultaneously encouraged innovation and left the brief deliberately rather open. Coates contributed ideas on a system of prefabrication in steel, concrete, glass and, characteristically, plywood. The

6. Curtis, *op.cit.* p.25.

7. Jill Lever interview, p.21.

8. 'Wells Coates: Recollections by Patrick Gwynne: April 1979', copy in Lasdun archive, p.2.

9. Sherban Cantacuzino, *Wells Coates: A Monograph*, London, Gordon Fraser, 1978, pp.75 and 64–71.

10. Interview with Alan Powers, November 1995.

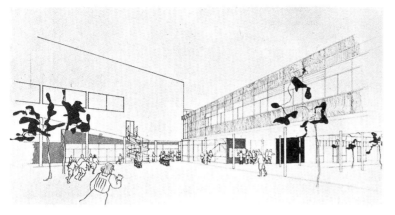

Figure 4. *News Chronicle* Schools Competition, 1937, Lasdun with Wells Coates.

11. *Architects' Journal*, vol.85, 25 March 1937, pp.530–31 and 536–7.

partitions would have offered negligible sound insulation, but the judges seem to have been more concerned that the layout of cloakrooms would mean that in poor weather 'some pupils would have to walk long distances inside the building in wet clothes'.[11]

Lasdun's scheme, like several of the others, was based on a spine block with components branching off it. He arranged the classroom corridors at right-angles to the spine, creating a series of landscaped courtyards open at one end to playing fields, and leading through *pilotis* at the other end to gardens. The overall layout was similar to the sort of Bauhaus-influenced diagrammatic schemes to which Lasdun was to become hostile after the war, proposing an alternative in buildings like his Hallfield School, Paddington. The landscaping and careful detailing, however, rendered the scheme human, open and welcoming. The charming sketches produced as part of the 1937 presentation show realistic children moving through corridors lined with their toys, and glimpses of murals and child art of the sort which was indeed to become a feature of the schools built immediately after the war, notably the pioneering series in Hertfordshire.

This first period of practice may well have taught Lasdun a number of useful lessons. Lasdun gave Coates generous credit in subsequent interviews for having shown him the importance of sectional planning, and of precision in detailing. Coates's quixotic utopianism may also have presented an instructive counter-example for an ambitious young architect: as Lasdun later recalled, 'most of the projects which he should have done probably collapsed because he frightened people about his tremendously advanced thoughts and macro-

Figure 5. *News Chronicle* Schools Competition, plan.

Figure 6. *News Chronicle* Schools Competition, aerial view.

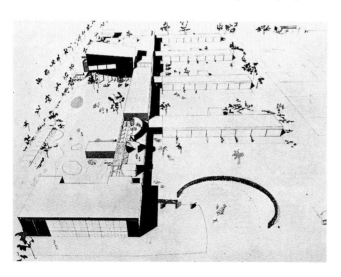
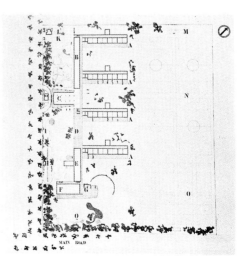

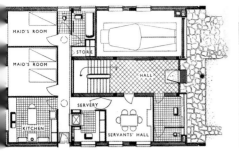   

scopic view of everything.'[12] Lasdun avoided scaring off clients in this manner, keeping a clear sense of the scope of projects in which he was engaged. He never sought to replace the entire city, but rather to improve it as much as he could within the restrictions of his site and brief. So well-grounded was he in realism that at UEA and the Christ's College residences he designed the first stages of multi-stage building projects to establish a language for future development by other architects if necessary. This has allowed both projects to retain their architectural quality in spite of remaining incomplete.

While he was still in Coates's office Lasdun gained another independent commission for a house. This time the client was an artist and a friend of Lasdun's mother, and the site was in Newton Road, Westbourne Park. Completed in 1938, the house is in a different world to that of Silver Greys. The conversion to Le Corbusier is very clear – indeed the façade is almost a paraphrase of the Maison Cook, which Lasdun had seen on his Paris visit – as is the great increase in confidence and skill which Lasdun's architecture had undergone in the intervening four years. It uses reinforced-concrete construction competently, thanks in part to the help of the engineer Felix Samuely, and is a unified, well-planned and well-detailed piece of 1930s modernism. Maxwell Fry wrote to Lasdun in 1939 to say that he had paid a number of visits to Newton Road, and felt that it was 'a real accession of strength to modern architecture'.[13]

The façade, with its white-painted concrete and chocolate tiles (currently painted an unhappy pastel yellow) is beautiful in the photos of the day. A gesture is made towards at least three of Le Corbusier's 'five points': the *fenêtre en longueur* in the strip windows, which can open to make a fourteen-foot clear opening; the *piloti* in the structurally unnecessary central column, and the roof garden in the small balcony on the top floor. Structurally it does not meet the Corbusian ideal of separating skeleton from walls, but this might be taken less as a failure of courage than as a victory of practical sense: since thick walls are needed for thermal and acoustic insulation, why not stand the building on them? Similarly the lighting internally, especially in the living room, is from a number of indirect sources, whereas Le Corbusier in his Purism lights from one or two exposed bulbs. Lasdun, in other words, rejects what he does not find admirable in his model, and keeps that which is desirable.

The other quiet divergence from the Corbusian ideal detectable in 32 Newton Road is Lasdun's concern for the location of his building. Whereas Le Corbusier tended to design for imagined green spaces irrespective of the surroundings, and his photographers used all their ingenuity in maintaining the illusion, Lasdun, even in 1937–8, was thinking about the relationship between his building and the street in which it stood. Thus the white concrete façade is not continued round to the side walls, which are instead of London stock brick, just as the neighbouring villas have a stucco front and brick sides. In terms of massing, too, Lasdun fought to be sympathetic to his surroundings, even at the cost of a five-month planning dispute. The house was to be considerably taller than its neighbours, so Lasdun set it as far back from the road as he was permitted, and also matched the tiled panel to the scale of the surrounding houses.

Figure 8. 32 Newton Road, plans.

12. Interview with Alan Powers, *op.cit.*

13. Letter from Maxwell Fry to Lasdun, 24 April 1939, Lasdun archive.

Figure 9. 32 Newton Road, Cartoonist Ronald Searle lived in the house after the original client, drawing this change of address card.

Figure 10. 32 Newton Road, balcony.
(RIBA Library Photographs Collection).

Figure 11. 32 Newton Road, living room
with client's antique furniture.
(RIBA Library Photographs Collection).

Figure 12. 32 Newton Road, living room
with Aalto furniture.
(RIBA Library Photographs Collection).

Internally, the planning is predominantly fairly conventional, with rooms disposed around a central staircase at the back of the house. The artist's studio which almost fills the top floor, and the L-shaped living and dining room are both attractive spaces, but there is little of the sectional virtuosity which Lasdun was to exhibit later in his career. This must be in part because of the nature of the commission, but it also seems likely that he had simply not yet developed that level of sophistication and skill as an architect.

An aspect of 32 Newton Road which demonstrates Lasdun's maturity at this time is the quality of its publicity. Whereas Silver Greys was little published, and when it was the photography was technically rather ordinary, Newton Road was widely and beautifully published, with first-class photographs, ample drawings, and, in the *Architectural Review* at least, visually impressive technical drawings extended from photographs to show details.[14] It seems likely that he had learnt much of this technique at Tecton, whose work was always sensationally presented, and with whom he was working at the time the publication of Newton Road was prepared. Two sets of interior photographs were taken, one with the client's collection of paintings and beautiful antiques in place, and the other with a selection of Aalto plywood furniture and strongly shaped pot plants which move from place to place to furnish each picture. This was used as an opportunity for the magazines to meditate on the use of antique and modern furniture in modern interiors, and indeed both look exceedingly attractive in the spare living room with its striking mid-Victorian marble fireplace.[15] This awareness of the critical importance of presentation and image quality to the success of an architect was to stand Lasdun in very good stead throughout his career. For his post-war projects he worked with top photographers (Donat, Einzig and others) and made extensive use of the marvellously intricate, expressive models produced from the 1960s onwards by his remarkable model maker Philip Wood.

14. *Architectural Review*, vol.85, March 1939, pp.119–32.

15. *Architect Building News*, 17 March 1939, pp.330–33; *Architectural Review*, vol.85, March 1939, pp.119–32.

Lasdun later stated that it was an attempt by Coates to poach the Newton Road commission from him which drove him to leave the office.[16] In any case there was insufficient interesting work for the firm by 1937, and finances were stretched. Just as Lasdun had essentially seen Coates as a surrogate Le Corbusier, so now he was attracted by Highpoint I, which Le Corbusier himself had warmly praised, to Lubetkin and Tecton. He made an appointment with Lubetkin, and impressed him with a white-on-black drawing of the Newton Road façade. Lasdun joined Tecton in 1937, and left to join the army in 1938, but he later spoke of this brief period as an exciting one, and a strong influence on him. His memories of the episode were not especially clear, perhaps in part because of confusions between his pre- and post-war work for the firm. He recalled sweeping the steps of Finsbury Health Centre before its opening, but seems to have joined the practice too late to be more architecturally involved in any of Tecton's most iconic 1930s work.[17]

What certainly did occupy much of his time with Lubetkin was work on the bombproof shelter schemes which Tecton drew up for the borough of Finsbury as the war approached.[18] One could speculate that the collaboration with Arup on the concrete design for these projects may have increased his knowledge of that material, or that his first taste of political obstruction in a major public project may have helped him to prepare for numerous such incidents later in his career, but it is hard to be confident. When Lasdun was demobbed he went back to Tecton as a partner – an indication that his talents had been appreciated during his first period with the firm.

Lasdun and Lubetkin formed a lasting respect for each other. Lasdun recalled that he 'came very close to Lubetkin … . I really enjoyed his company enormously.'[19] Although the end of Tecton caused bad feeling, and Lubetkin's retreat to rural isolation left them out of contact for decades, Lasdun repeatedly proposed Lubetkin for the RIBA Royal Gold Medal in the 1970s and 1980s, eventually successfully, and Lubetkin was grateful and touched by this solidarity. He wrote to Lasdun: 'you have deservedly flown to such olympic heights that I hesitated to inflict myself upon you. Yet it is obvious that all the time you were busy on my behalf organising the forthcoming exhumation ceremony.'[20]

With Lasdun's departure from Tecton in 1938, the story of his pre-war architecture ends. There remains the question of what impact his pre-war work had on his more famous buildings of the 1950s and 1960s. He learnt practical lessons and developed an attitude to the role of the architect. He also absorbed several of the influences which were to shape his later work.

Undoubtedly Lasdun had acquired, from Silver Greys onwards, a much more extensive experience of the practicalities of design and construction than most architects of his age. He had worked with two firms which used reinforced concrete confidently and stylishly, and with both Arup and Samuely – the two leading architectural engineers then practising in Britain. He had also seen at first hand the workings of two artistically ambitious leading architects, and had doubtless observed the strengths and weaknesses of their methods of directing the design process. Certainly Coates, Lubetkin and Lasdun, although all competent draughtsmen, each did very little drawing at the height of their careers. Each sketched to demonstrate points, and talked to their assistants, but designed substantially with the hands of others. Each kept their teams small and selected associates with great care. Lasdun's comparison of Coates's role with that of an orchestral conductor would do well for his own creative process too.

Although Lasdun felt he was 'not a political animal', he took to heart the idea that 'architecture was nothing to do with styles, it was to do with society and social requirements' – an idea first put to him by Herbert J. Rowse at the AA, and much reinforced by the utopias, technological and socialistic, for which Coates and Lubetkin fought.[21] He truly believed in the Welfare State which was the client for much of his greatest work.

16. Jill Lever interview, p.23.

17. Jill Lever interview, p.30.

18. Jill Lever interview, p.29.

19. Jill Lever interview, p.30.

20. Letter from Berthold Lubetkin to Lasdun, 9 March 1982, Lasdun archive.

21. Jill Lever interview, pp.33 and 16.

Looking back to the 1930s from the perspective of the 1990s Lasdun found the roots of much which was later to develop in his creative process. There was of course the influence of Le Corbusier, acquired young and retained thereafter, shifting in the post-war period to accommodate the earthier style of the Unité d'Habitation, the Maisons Jaoul and above all La Tourette. Lasdun also acquired his admiration for Hawksmoor at the AA, producing a measured drawing of his Kensington orangery. Another influence which Lasdun acknowledged late in life was the role of S. Rowland Pierce at the AA in introducing him to the importance of Lutyens's connecting spaces – staircases, halls, etc.[22] Combined with the Corbusian and Beaux-Arts notion of the *promenade architecturale*, the three-dimensional experience of moving through a building was to become ever more important to Lasdun in his post-war work, with 'processional routes' shaping the National Theatre foyers, the Royal College of Physicians and the European Investment Bank in Luxembourg.

His awakening with Coates to the potential of sectional sophistication in

Figure 13. Royal College of Physicians, 1959–63. (RIBA Library Photographs Collection).

Figure 14. National Theatre, 1967–76.
(RIBA Library Photographs Collection).

design was also to lead to fruitful development in later work. At one level this was used in the way that Coates had used it – to achieve higher densities with a jigsaw-like ingenuity. This is clearest in the student room planning at UEA and Christ's, in which the complex interlocking floors were detailed by Ted Cullinan to pack a maximum of south-facing accommodation into a minimum rise.[23] At another level, Lasdun's skill in designing through several floors at once was to become a potent artistic tool. Although it was to be the late 1950s before this really bore fruit, the creation of his best buildings was done almost entirely through models, as drawings were inadequate to visualise the effect of complex spaces over several floors. In his later work, Lasdun would sometimes take a model outside covered in black cloth and peer in to see how the light would fall in the space when built.[24] In the later 1930s, however, he was still some way from this level of dedication to spatial effect. Newton Road is clearly a house designed on a drawing board: it has a flat façade, and a series of well-planned but relatively straightforward floors. It is instantly legible from four plans and one elevation, whereas to comprehend any of the major post-war designs from drawings alone takes serious time and effort.

By the time he went to war, Lasdun had come a long way in a short while. He had acquired experience, ambition and skill as an architect, as well as reputation and contacts. After seven years of reflection on architecture during his army service, Lasdun returned to practice. He took a prominent role in the last years of CIAM, and gained more experience building both in London with Tecton, and in Ghana. With his experience, talent, skilful handling of committees, devotion to establishing a faithful brief through dialogue with the client, and sheer drive, he was poised for the highest success. Less than a decade older than Peter Smithson or James Stirling, and only 11 years older than Robert Venturi, he had had contact with a pre-war architectural world which for them was essentially history. When, in 1959, he established Denys Lasdun and Partners, he was for several years the most sought-after and respected architect in the country, landing within five years commissions for a new university, the Royal College of Physicians, the National Theatre, and a new college and other buildings for Cambridge, and turning down numerous other prestigious projects for lack of time. The 1930s were only the beginning for Lasdun – an education – but they were a good education.

22. Lasdun talk given to Twentieth Century Society, 1999.

23. Author's interview with Ted Cullinan, summer 2004.

24. Jill Lever interview, p.56.

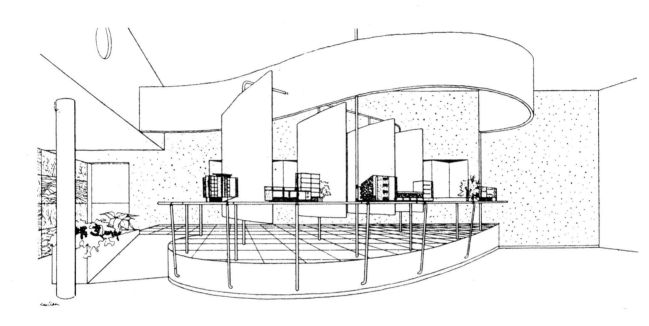

MARS Group exhibition 1938, drawing by Gordon Cullen